Canadian Society

Rudy Fenwick

The Association for Canadian Studies in the United States
(ACSUS)

The Association for Canadian Studies in the United States (ACSUS), founded in 1971, is a multidisciplinary academic organization devoted to encouraging and supporting the study of Canada and the Canada-United States relationship in all its facets. ACSUS publishes a quarterly scholarly journal, The American Review of Canadian Studies, a regular newsletter, Canadian Studies Update, and hosts a biennial conference atrracting over 600 participants. ACSUS is the largest association of Canadian Studies specialists in the world.

Also published by ACSUS:

Northern Exposures: Scholarship on Canada in the United States, edited by Karen L. Gould, Joseph T. Jockel, and William Metcalfe (1993) ISBN 1-883027-00-4

Acknowledgment

The ACSUS Papers were conceived to provide suitable core materials for introductory college courses and solid background material for more focused courses on Canada for undergraduates in the United States. The first edition, published in 1989, was extremely successful in serving this market. The concept of the series has withstood the test of time and ACSUS is pleased to cooperate with Michigan State University Press on this second edition.

This edition was made possible with the assistance of the Government of Canada/*avec l'aide du Gouvernement du Canada.*

Editors:

Joseph T. Jockel
St. Lawrence University

Victor M. Howard
Michigan State University

Introduction

Like other advanced industrial countries, Canada has an urban, educated, healthy, and affluent population that enjoys one of the highest standards of living in the world. Canada also is plagued by many of the problems that are all too typical of the developed world, such as pollution, crime, drug use, and the persistence of poverty. Nonetheless, it has been an open question whether Canadians, unlike their counterparts in most other industrial countries, constitute a true "society" in the sociological meaning of the term, and are not just an aggregate of people living in the same geographical space within the same political boundaries.

Sociologists maintain that a true society has, first, a set of institutions, values, and norms supporting a subjective identify different from that of other societies; and second, some degree of internal cohesion with respect to these characteristics. Although most countries periodically face problems in maintaining their identity and internal cohesion, history and geography have conspired to make both problems more acute and more continuous in the case of Canada.

A distinct Canadian identity was slow to emerge because many Canadians were reluctant to sever ties with Britain. Canada's identity and national cohesion are made even more problematic by its relatively small, geographically dispersed, and culturally heterogeneous population. Indeed, it may be more appropriate to describe Canada as not one but two societies—English and French. Since the British conquest of New France (Quebec) in 1759, Canada has had to face the problem of integrating not only two languages but two religions and two cultures with two visions of nationhood. Added to this division is the great diversity of ethnic groups within English (or more appropriately "non-French") Canada, as well as regional differences in economic activities.

The geographic proximity of the United States had a decisive influence on Canada. To be sure, the two countries boast of having the world's longest undefended border, across which people, goods, capital, and culture flow freely. However, from Canada's perspective, such a close, friendly relationship with the "giant next door" is not all to the good. Many Canadians fear their country has become so inundated by American culture and so economically intertwined with the United States that not only is their identity threatened, but their national sovereignty is undermined.

Everywhere in the world, geography and climate help determine where people will live, how they will interact with one another, and what kind of economic

1

activities they will pursue. Canadian geography—the rugged Atlantic and Pacific coastlines, the norhtern tundra, the Canadian Shield, and the Rocky Mountains—has often made transportation and communication easier between north and south than between east and west. As a result, ties between Canadian and American regions have been encouraged (for example between the prairie provinces and Great Plains states, or between Atlantic Canada and New England), while communication between Canadian regions has been hindered. This situation, in turn, has helped to produce strong Canadian regional identities, which have been strengthened by social forces, including economic and political policies.

This monograph discusses the forces that have shaped contemporary Canadian society. In the next section, we use census and social indicators to examine basic social characteristics and processes such as population change and distribution, health and illness, family and crime. We also look at socioeconomic characteristics, such as occupational and industrial makeup, education levels, and income distribution. Then we examine the problem of cohesion in Canadian society in more detail, presenting data on the cultural heterogeneity of the Canadian population and looking further at the French-English conflict and regionalism within English Canada. The issue of Canadian identity is also explored more fully; we look at the extent to which Canadian institutions and values are unique and were developed consciously in reaction to American institutions and values. We also examine the questions of foreign ownership and the penetration of American culture—especially via the media—into Canada. The final section presents our conclusions about whether Canada constitutes a society in the sociological sense of the term.

A Social Portrait of Canada

This section presents an overview of the fundamental characteristics of the Canadian population, making comparisons whenever possible with the population characteristics of other industrialized countries, especially the United States.

Population

Distribution and Trends

As of 1992, Canada's total population was estimated at 27,402,000, making it the thirty-first most populous country in the world. This population inhabited a territory of 3,851,787 square miles, the second largest territory, after Russia. In contrast, the population of the United States in 1992 was approximately ten times that of Canada but inhabited a somewhat smaller land area. Indicative of the difference in land size is the fact that the distance between St. John's, Newfoundland, on the Atlantic, to Victoria, British Columbia, on the Pacific, is over five hundred miles greater than the distance between Boston and Los Angeles. Indeed, St. John's is closer to Dublin, Ireland than it is to Chicago. There are approximately 7.1 Canadians per square mile; in comparison, the United States has approximately 70 persons per square mile, while the world average is approximately 100 persons per square mile.

Perhaps the most important fact about the Canadian population, however, is its uneven dispersion over its vast territory. Because of severe climatic conditions and geography, such as the northern tundra and the Canadian, or Pre-Cambrian, Shield that runs through northern Quebec and Ontario, much of Canada's northern expanses are uninhabitable. In fact, no permanent human settlement is found in approximately 89 percent of Canada's land area. The majority of the population is concentrated in a more or less unbroken band within two hundred miles of the U.S. border, while the combined population of the two vast northern territories (the Yukon and the Northwest Territories) amounts to only about 84,000—0.3 percent of Canada's total population. As of the last official census in 1981, a majority of Canadians lived in the two provinces of Ontario and Quebec (see table 1). Over one-third of all Canadians live in Ontario, while just over a quarter call Quebec home. Moreover, most of the population of these two provinces live in the "Golden Triangle" that runs from Quebec City southwest through Montreal and Toronto to Windsor, on the Detroit River, north to Sault Ste. Marie, then east through Ottawa and back to Quebec City. Within this triangle lies the industrial heartland of Canada, along the shores of the Great Lakes, as well as the fertile farmlands of southern Ontario and the St. Lawrence River Valley. At the other extreme, aside from the Yukon and Northwest Territories, less than 1 percent of Canada's population lives in the Atlantic province of Prince Edward Island.

Table 1

The Population Distribution of Canada, 1951, 1981 and 1992

(percentage)

Province or Territory	1951	1981	1992	Population in 1992
Newfoundland	2.6%	2.3%	2.1%	578,000
Prince Edward Island	0.7	0.5	0.5	130,000
Nova Scotia	4.6	3.5	3.2	906,000
New Brunswick	3.7	2.9	2.7	729,000
Quebec	28.9	26.4	25.3	6,925,000
Ontario	32.8	35.4	36.9	10,099,000
Manitoba	5.5	4.2	4.0	1,097,000
Saskatchewan	5.9	4.8	3.6	993,000
Alberta	6.7	9.2	9.4	2,563,000
British Columbia	8.3	11.3	12.0	3,298,000
Yukon	0.1	0.1	0.1	28,000
Northwest Territories	0.1	0.1	0.2	56,000
Total	100.0%	100.0%	100.0%	27,402,000[a]

Source: *Canada Year Book 1994* (Ottawa: Statistics Canada, 1994), 112.

[a] Column does not add to total because of rounding.

Not surprisingly, the greatest population densities are found in Canadian cities, especially the two largest, Montreal and Toronto, which average more than 8,000 persons per square mile. Overall, 75.7 percent of Canada's population lives in an urban environment, which is approximately the same as the percentage of urban-dwelling Americans. The degree of urbanization ranges from 36.3 percent in Prince Edward Island to 86.3 percent in Ontario. British Columbia also has more than three-quarters of its population living in urban areas (77.9 percent), while only Prince Edward Island and the Northwest Territories have larger rural than urban populations. In New Brunswick the rural and urban populations are about equal.

In recent years, two trends in the population distribution for Canada and the United States have appeared to indicate a transition from industrial to postindustrial societies. First, in both countries during the 1970s the rural population grew faster than the urban population. In Canada, between 1976 and 1981, the urban population grew by 5 percent, while the rural population grew by 8.9 percent. In the United States, between 1970 and 1980, the rural population grew 15 percent compared with 10 percent for the urban population. Moreover, much of this rural growth in both countries came from the migration of urban residents to the countryside.

What is behind this "rural renaissance" in North America? Clearly, the answer is not any increased desire of North Americans to farm the land; indeed, the number of farms in both countries continued to decline. Rather, this pattern of rural growth stems from several developments. Developments in transportation have allowed people to live and commute farther from their jobs in cities, while developments in communications have allowed these new rural residents to keep in touch with urban cultural life. Second, earlier retirement ages and better pension plans have allowed older people to move closer to and take greater advantage of recreational facilities that are found mainly in rural areas. Third, and perhaps most important, the countryside is where industrial growth is occurring. Older industries are taking advantage of the better transportation and communication to escape the higher land, labor, and tax costs of urban areas. In addition, many of the new growth industries, particularly recreation and energy, are, by their nature, located in rural areas.

The ability of people and industry to escape older, high-density urban areas and the growth of new service industries also figure in the second trend: the westward (and southward in the United States) movement of the North American population. Historically, Canadians and Americans have been among the most geographically mobile peoples of the world, a characteristic that appears to be a legacy of the settlement of their frontiers. As is the case with most voluntary population movements, those in North America have been motivated by the search for better living standards and a higher quality of life. And because these goals are determined primarily by economic opportunities, the main pattern of movement has been from economically disadvantaged regions to regions enjoying economic prosperity and growth. As the heavy manufacturing industries in the old Rust Belt cities along the Atlantic coast and Great Lakes have declined and the service, high-tech, and energy industries in the Sun Belt regions of the American south and American and Canadian West have expanded, it is not surprising that the populations of the United States and Canada have made the same migration during the past generation.

The westward population movement in Canada is clearly shown in table 1. Although no province or territory lost population between 1951 and 1991, all provinces east of Ontario show declines in their shares of Canada's total population, as do the prairie provinces of Manitoba and Saskatchewan. Ontario's share of the population grew during this period, but less rapidly than did the western provinces of Alberta and British Columbia. Most of the growth in these western provinces has been the result of migration from other provinces, rather than natural population increase (i.e., surplus of births over deaths). Furthermore, all provinces east of Alberta, including Ontario, suffered net migration losses between 1971 and 1991; only Ontario was an exception to this pattern in the previous decade.

Alberta's population growth has been attributed largely to its energy boom and resultant economic growth in the late 1970s. Indeed, there is evidence that Alberta has suffered net migration losses in the 1980s, due primarily to the economic effects of the 1982 recession along with the worldwide slump in energy prices that persisted during the 1980s.

Also worth noting in table 1 is the decline in Quebec's population share between 1951 and 1991 (from 28.9 percent to 25.3 percent). The reasons were twofold: the declining birthrate among French Quebecers during the 1950s and 1960s (from the highest to lowest rates of any group in Canada) and the increased out-migration of Quebecers (especially non-Francophones) during the 1970s. Quebec's net out-migration increased from 21,131 persons between 1971 and 1976 to 62,264 between 1976 and 1981. This accelerated out-migrationn has been attributed to concerns among non-Francophone Quebecers regarding changes in the provincial language policies designed to foster the French language and the threat of separation from Canada.

To put some perspective on these recent trends in population movement it is necessary to look at the long-term demographic trends as well as the overall population structure. Population growth is determined by two demographic factors: natural increase (the excess of births over deaths) and net migration (immigration minus emigration). As is shown in table 2, Canada's population growth rate has fluctuated considerably since the middle of the nineteenth century. For example, during the last decade of the nineteenth century the average annual rate of growth was only 1.1 percent, but in the first decade of the twentieth century Canada's annual population growth rate was 3 percent, its highest ever. The lowest average annual growth rate occurred during the 1930s, when it was only 1 percent. In general, these fluctuations in population growth rates correspond with economic cycles: growth rates are high in times of economic prosperity, as in the first decade of the twentieth century, and low in economic hard times, as in the 1890s and 1930s. Obviously, families can afford to have more children

6

during times of prosperity, and prosperity encourages immigration by increasing the demand for labor. Conversely, economic recessions or depressions reduce the financial ability to have children as well as discourage immigration by reducing labor demand. During economic downturns, Canada also experiences increased levels of emigration, primarily to the United States. This demographic force, which accounts for small population change in the United States, has great significance for demographic change in Canada.

Table 2.

Total Population Growth in Canada, Selected years, 1851-1991

Census Year	Population	Increase between Censuses (%)	Average annual rate of growth (%)
1851	2,436,297	——	——
1861	3,229,633	32.6%	2.9%
1871	3,689,257	14.2	1.3
1881	4,324,810	17.2	1.6
1891	4,833,239	11.8	1.1
1901	5,371,315	11.1	1.1
1911	7,206,643	34.2	3.0
1921	8,787,949	21.9	2.0
1931	10,376,786	18.1	1.7
1941	11,506,655	10.9	1.0
1951	14,009,429	21.8	1.7
1961	18,238,247	30.2	2.8
1971	21,568,311	18.3	1.6
1981	24,343,181	8.9	1.2
1991	27,108,000	11.4	1.5

Source: Statistics Canada, *Canada Year Book 1994* (Ottawa: Statistics Canada, 1994), 112-13, tables 3.2 and 3.3.

The population of Canada has more than doubled since World War II (see table 2). The baby boom in the 1950s corresponded with a long period of economic growth in North America. But that growth rate began to decline in the relatively prospering 1960s and by 1981 had fallen to 1.1 percent. It increased slightly to 1.5 percent by 1991. Although this is the highest growth rate in the industrial world, it is only half of Canada's rate in 1961. However, rather than economic causes, the slowing of population growth in the past quarter century appears more attributable to changing social values that placed greater emphasis on small families (especially in French Quebec), increased labor force participation among women of childbearing years, and increased concern with quality of life and the resulting consciousness of the harmful effects of overpopulation.

Natural increase has accounted for approximately 80 percent of Canada's population growth in recent years. The annual rate of natural increase in 1991 was 8 per 1,000 population, which, although one of the highest rates among industrial countries, is the lowest in Canadian history. Over the past decade, the actual number of live births in Canada has risen slightly because of the increase in the number of women in their childbearing years. The overall birthrate, which fell to 15 per 1,000 in 1985, increased to 18 per 1,000 in 1991. However, without an even greater increase in the birthrate, demographers project that Canada will experience a population decline early in the next century.

The rest of Canada's recent population growth is accounted for by net immigration. As in other white-settler, frontier societies, such as the United States, Australia, Argentina, and New Zealand, immigration has historically played a significant role in Canada's population growth. According to the 1981 census, one in six Canadians reported having been born outside the country. But, immigration to Canada diminished as employment opportunities decreased, during the 1970s and 1980s; moreover, as a response to the economic recession of the early 1980s, the Canadian government cut the number of immigrants who could enter Canada to fewer than 100,000 per year.

Until the 1970s, the majority of immigrants to Canada came from European countries, especially the British Isles, but in the past decade the diversity in the origins of immigrants has increased. Although European immigrants continue to make up a substantial percentage of all those settling in Canada, many immigrants now are coming from countries in the Third World—Asia, Africa, and Latin America.

Increasingly restrictive immigration policies have also raised the average age of immigrants coming to Canada, because the new restrictions are aimed at "independent" immigrants—those who have no family already residing in Canada—most of whom are young adults. No new restrictions were placed on immigrants entering Canada for "family reunification"—those already having families in Canada—most of whom are older adults. In 1970, the average age was 25.5 years for men and 26.3 for women. By 1983, it had increased to 30.9 years for men and 32.7 for women.

8

Aging

Although Canada is still a comparatively young country, with an average age of around thirty-two years in 1991, it is aging rapidly as life expectancy increases and the birthrate declines. For example, the proportion of all Canadians whose age is fifteen years or under dropped from 34 percent in 1961 to 21 percent in 1991 and is projected to be approximately 17 percent by 2001. In contrast, the proportion of Canadians age sixty five and above increased from 8 percent in 1961 to 12 percent in 1991 and is expected to be around 14 percent by 2001.

As Canada's population ages, the overall proportion of women to men increases because women have a longer life expectancy than men, 80 years versus 74 years. Almost 58 percent of Canadians age sixty five and above in 1991 were women (as opposed to slightly below 50 percent among persons age fifteen years old and younger). Moreover, 60 percent of these older women are widowed, divorced, or never married.

Similar trends in age and sex structures of populations are causing problems throughout the industrial world. The rapidity of population aging is already forcing countries like Canada and the United States to make social and economic adjustments. Policymakers are particularly concerned about increased health care costs required by an older population and increased pressure on pension or retirement systems. As the proportion of persons of retirement age increases, relatively fewer workers will be paying into public pension funds or social security and relatively more retirees will be drawing on them. Without significant alterations in pension system, some policy planners foresee increasingly acute pension "crisis" in the next century.

Family Structure

As is true of other industrial countries, aging of the population has reduced the percentage of the Canadian population in the prime marriage years (late teens to early thirties) and so the marriage rate has declined. In 1991, there were 7 marriages per 1,000 population in Canada, down 5 percent from 1985. Average age at first marriage also continues to increase, up to 25 years for brides and 27 years for bridegrooms in 1991, from 23.5 and 25.7 years, respectively, in 1981. By comparison, Americans marry slightly more often (9.5 per 1,000 in 1990) and at younger ages, 23 years for brides and 25 for grooms, as of 1990. However, U.S. marriage trends are headed in the same direction as those in Canada.

A more significant difference between Canadian and American families concerns divorce rates. Canadians divorce only half as often as Americans: 2.9 per

1,000 population in 1991 versus 4.7 per 1,000 in the United States. For both countries, these figures represent dramatic increases over the past quarter-century. In 1951, the American divorce rate was 2.3, while the Canadian rate was only 0.38; in 1981, those rates were 5.3 and 2.8, respectively. Some observers have argued that the lower divorce rates in Canada are indicative of a more conservative, traditional value system, with less emphasis on individualism. Others argue that the lower divorce rates in Canada are attributable to its later liberalization of divorce laws—after 1968.

Other changes in Canadian family structure are worth noting, although all are similar to changes occurring in other countries. Declining birthrates are reflected in ever-smaller families, averaging 3.1 members by 1991. Economic and occupational changes have increased labor force participation among women, especially married women (a trend that is discussed in detail later). Also, the number of single-parent families has increased by almost a third during the 1980s, from 9.8 percent of all families in 1981 to 13 percent in 1991. Moreover, eight in ten of these single-parent families are headed by women. As in the United States, this trend has been cause for concern, because such families are more likely to be poor.

Health and Health Care

Despite its overall aging, Canada's population is one of the world's healthiest, and it is getting healthier. In the early 1990s, Canada's mortality rate stood at a record low of 6.8 per 1,000 population. As already mentioned, life expectancy continues to increase into the seventies and beyond for both men and women. As in the United States, this increasing longevity is generally attributed to medical advances in the treatment of the leading cause of death in North America—cardiovascular diseases.

Cardiovascular diseases claim the lives of 50 more Canadians than are claimed by cancer, the second leading cause of death (283 per 100,000 population compared with 197 per 100,000). Far fewer deaths are attributable to the next three leading killers: respiratory diseases (61 per 100,000), accident (49 per 100,000), and diabetes (12). These rates are comparable to those found in the American population, as is the order in which they kill. The figures for 1991 are down sharply from those only ten years before. For example, deaths from heart disease are down 30 percent; from stroke down 39 percent; from accidents down 27 percent. The exception is mortality from cancer, which increased 4 percent; this increase stems from a 95 percent increase in mortality rates from lung cancer among women, which is probably attributable to the increased number of women smokers.

10

Infant mortality is often used as an indicator of a nation's health and its health care system, because it is a condition that can be reduced with better and more accessible health care. In 1991, Canada's infant mortality rate was 7 per 1,000 live births, thirteenth lowest of any nation, after Sweden. In contrast, the United States with a rate of 9.2, ranked sixteenth. As with other industrial nations, current figures represent a dramatic decline in infant mortality during the twentieth century. In 1921, the first year for which such statistics are available, Canada's infant mortality rate was 102.1.

If the quality of Canadian health care has increased, so have its costs—to the point that cost has become the most significant health care problem (excluding the potential effects of AIDS). In 1991 Canada spent 10 percent of its gross domestic product (GDP) on health care ($2,474 per capital). By comparison, the United States spent 12 percent of its gross national product (GNP) on health care ($2,869 per capita). In 1970, in contrast, health care cost Canada 7.1 percent of its GDP ($293 per capita), while it cost the United States 7.7 percent of its GNP ($324 per capita). During this period, the greatest and the fastest-rising health care costs have been for hospitals.

Despite the similarities between Canada and the United States in health and health care, there is one substantial difference. Canada has a universal, prepaid, national health insurance program under which physicians, fees and most hospital costs are paid by the government. The system is supported by taxes and premiums collected by the federal and provincial governments. Responsibility for providing health care rests with each province or territory; these governments pay roughly half the cost and the federal government the remaining half. Overall, the government pays 72 percent of the total health care bill in Canada, compared with about 40 percent in the United States.

Crime

Crime statistics provide another indicator of the overall well-being of a population. Using these statistics, many observers argue that Canadians are relatively safe from crime, especially when compared with the American population. Certainly, when it comes to violent crimes, such as murder and armed robbery, Canada's crime rates are substantially lower than those in the United States. In 1991, there were 2.1 murders and 121 robberies committed for every 100,000 Canadians, compared with 9 murders and 209 robberies for every 100,000 Americans.

When the rates for nonviolent property crimes are compared, however, the differences are far less substantial. In 1985, there were 324 auto thefts in Canada per

100,000 population versus 462 per 100,000 in the United States. And the rate for burglary (breaking and entering) is actually higher in Canada: 1,407 per 100,000 versus 1,287 in the United States. Moreover, as with divorce rates, differences in Canadian-U.S. crime rates are narrowing somewhat. During the 1980s, the murder rate increased by 8 percent in Canada, whereas it actually declined slightly in the United States. Overall, violent crimes were up 29.8 percent in Canada during this period, but down 2 percent in the United States. Similarly, property crimes were up 12.8 percent in Canada, but down 3.4 percent in the United States.

As with the earlier comparison of divorce rates, it has been argued that Canada has a more "law and order" culture thanks to its British legacy of deference to authority (including the law), conservatism and traditionalism. But such value differences do not account for the lack of difference in rates of property crime or in the declining differences in overall crime rates. Do these trends indicate an "Americanization" of Canadian culture? Alternative explanations, while not incompatible with the value-difference thesis, have stressed specific historical differences between the two countries. These include open racial conflict and the greater availability of firearms in the United States, along with the absence of vigilantism in the development of the Canadian frontier and the greater centralization of Canadian law enforcement under the Royal Canadian Mounted Police. These arguments are explored in more detail later in the discussion of the Canadian identity.

Socioeconomic Distributions and Trends

Occupational and Industrial Structures

Among industrial countries, three significant labor force changes have marked the path of economic development in the twentieth century: the increased participation of women in the labor force, the shift from agricultural to nonagricultural occupations, and the shift from industrial manufacturing to "post-industrial" service occupations.

Changes in the Canadian labor force participation rates for both sexes through the twentieth century are shown in table 3. As the table indicates, the male participation rate has always exceeded the female rate, but the difference has been steadily declining. Because these figures include age groups in which most members are still in school (15 through 24 years) or are retired (sixty five and older), the table suggests that virtually all males who are not in school or retired participate—that is, they are self-employed, employed outside the home, temporarily laid off, or in search of employment. The steady decline in male participation

12

rates (from almost 90 percent in 1911 to just over 74.8 percent in 1991) is due both to increasing attendance in colleges and universities, which delays entry into the labor force, and to the aging of the population already discussed (increasing life spans and lower retirement age mean more retired men in the population).

Table 3
Labor Force Participation of Males and Females, 15 Years Old and Older,
Canada, Selected Years, 1911-1991

Year	Males	Females
1911	89.6%	16.2%
1921	88.7	17.6
1931	87.5	19.6
1941	78.4	20.7
1951	83.8	24.1
1961	77.7	29.5
1971	75.7	39.2
1981	78.4	51.7
1991	73.8	57.6

Sources: Percentages years 1911 through 1971 are from the 1971 Census of Canada, Cat. 94-702. Percentages for 1981 are from *Canada Yearbook*, 1985. Percentages for 1991 are from *Canada Year Book*, 1994.

The more significant trend is the increase in female participation, from 16.2 percent in 1911 to more than 58.2 percent by 1991. There is every indication that this upward trend will continue. For example, as of 1991, the rate of labor force participation for females ages fifteen through twenty four was 65.1 percent, which is only 4 percent lower than the participation rate of males in this age group. In contrast, among women age twenty five and above, the participation rate was only 56.8 percent, a full twenty percentage points below the participation rate of men aged twenty five and older.

A number of factors have contributed to increased participation of women in the labor force: changes in values concerning the role of women in society; the effects of lower birthrates in freeing many women from child and child-rearing duties; the increasing number of single, divorced, and widowed women in the population; and the increasing economic desirability or necessity of having dual-career families. This last reason may explain why an increasing majority of women now in the labor force are married: 65 percent in 1991, compared with only 12.7 percent in 1941. Conversely, the percentage of working women who are single declined from 80 percent in 1941 to 29 percent in 1991.

Perhaps the most significant reason for increased female participation is long-term changes in occupational structure. Employment has moved away from jobs that were held almost exclusively by men, such as agriculture, toward jobs that have always had high levels of female participation, such as clerical or service occupations. These changes are chronicled in table 4. In 1901, agriculture was the single largest occupation in Canada, employing four in ten Canadian workers. By 1991, that figure was less than one in twenty. In contrast, white collar occupations have experienced substantial growth, especially in the professional and clerical categories. Professional occupations have increased from 4.6 percent to 18.2 percent since 1901, while clerical occupations have increased from 3.2 percent to 16.5 percent. Overall, by the 1990s, more than half of all Canadian workers held white-collar jobs.

The changes that have occurred in the other two major occupational categories—blue collar (or manual) workers and service workers—are especially relevant to predictions concerning the supposed transition from industrial to postindustrial society. According to these predictions, automated production technologies increasingly will reduce the need for blue-collar manufacturing workers, while rising affluence will increase the demand for all types of services—and for the workers to provide them. The trends depicted in table 4 somewhat support these predictions. The percentage of Canadian workers classified as blue-collar declined from 34.3 percent in 1961 to 24 percent in 1991. Before 1961, that percentage had remained at a fairly constant one-third of the labor force. At the same time the percentage of service workers has been steadily increasing from 8.2 percent in 1901 to 13.3 percent in 1991. Despite these changes, however, blue-collar workers continue to outnumber service workers in the Canadian labor force almost two to one.

As defined by the Canadian (or U.S.) census, the category of service occupations encompasses diverse jobs such as personal services, like domestics, along with workers such as hotel and restaurant workers. However, the service industries also employ a more inclusive category of workers, many of whom are classified as having white-collar jobs, such as bank tellers, teachers, entertainers, and social workers, and some of whom are classified as blue-collar, such as police and linemen for phone companies.

14

Table 4
Occupational Changes in Canada, 1901, 1961, and 1991

Occupation	1901	1961	1991	% Change, 1901-199
White-collar	*15.3%*	*39.9%*	*57.8%*	*42.5%*
Managerial, administrative	4.2	7.8	13.5	+ 9.3
Professional	.6	9.8	18.2	+ 13.6
Clerical	.2	13.7	16.5	+ 13.3
Sales	.1	8.6	9.7	+ 6.6
Blue-collar (Secondary industries)	*2.2*	*34.9*	*24.0*	*- 8.2*
Primary Industries	*4.3*	*12.8*	*4.9*	*-39.4*
Agriculture	0.3	10.0	3.7	-36.6
Other (fishing, trapping, etc. logging, mining, quarrying)	4.0	2.8	1.2	- 2.8
Service	*8.2*	*12.4*	*13.3*	*+ 5.1*
Total:	100.0%	100.0%	100.0%	

Sources: For 1901 and 1961, Alfred A. Hunter, "Class and Status in Canada," in *Introduction to Canadian Society: A Sociological Analysis*, eds. G.N. Ramu and Stuart D. Johnson. (Toronto: Maguillan, 1974), 120, table 2. For 1991, *Canada Year Book 1994*, 271, table 6.6.

Service industries are equivalent to what economists refer to as the tertiary sector of the economy. Other sectors are the primary, which is equivalent to extractive industries, such as farming and mining, and the secondary, or transformative, which is equivalent to manufacturing industries. The tertiary sector encompasses all other economic activities: commerce, transportation, communication, and various types of services, including all public services provided by government. When employment is determined by industry of employment rather than by type of job skills, more than 60 percent of Canadian workers are employed in service, or tertiary, industries. The breakdown of employment by industrial sector is provided in table 5.

Table 5 also provides information for comparing industrial and employment changes during the twentieth century in Canada with changes in other industrial countries. The classic model of industrial change predicts that economic development involves a transition first from extractive activities (preindustrial) to transformative activities (industrial), followed by a second transition to service activities (postindustrial). Although the information in this table does not go back far enough to capture completely the first transition in some countries, especially England, it does suggest that none of these industrial countries has followed this pattern of change exactly. Rather, the decline of employment in extractive industries has led to a growth of *both* transformative *and* service sector employment, especially in the European countries examined. By the 1970s, employment outside the extractive sector in these countries was evenly divided between the transformative and service sectors.

The pattern of industrial change in Canada has been very similar to that of the United States. In contrast to Europe in the 1920s, the North American countries already had a higher percentage of employment in service industries than in transformative industries, and this gap has widened significantly ever since. By 1970, employment in the service sector was nearly double that for the transformative sector in both countries. Whereas these trends conform to generalizations that industrial countries are moving toward a service based economy, corresponding predictions concerning the decline of the transformative sector (i.e., manufacturing) had not yet materialized to any significant degree in any of these countries.

Why should Canada and the United States have such large service sectors in comparison with European countries? Most explanations take into account the relatively high per capita incomes that have historically characterized economies of Canada and the United States. As already indicated, service sector employment is related to a country's level of affluence, one measure of which is per capita income. The reasons for high per capita incomes in North America are rooted in the white settler, frontier nature of their social and economic development. Small populations relative to the large amounts of productive, sparsely settled land helped maintain comparatively high wage levels as well as keep down the costs of necessities. Because food and other raw materials were abundant, they were relatively cheap. And because of the relative underpopulation, especially during the nineteenth century, North American industry had to depend on a more highly skilled, and thus more highly paid, labor force than was the case in European countries. This reliance on a highly skilled work force also meant that fewer workers were needed, particularly in manufacturing—a fact reflected in the smaller percentage of North Americans than Europeans employed in the transformative sector.

Table 5

Percentage Distribution of Labor Force Employment by Industry Sectors
for Six Industrial Countries, 1920, 1950, and 1970

Sector and Country	About 1920	About 1950	About 1970
Extractive			
Canada	36.9%	21.6%	9.1%
United States	28.9	14.4	4.5
England	14.2	8.9	4.2
Germany	33.5	16.1	5.1
France	43.6	31.9	17.0
Japan	56.3	50.3	20.0
Transformative			
Canada	26.1	33.7	30.0
United States	32.9	33.9	33.9
England	42.2	45.4	43.8
Germany	38.9	47.3	49.0
France	29.7	35.2	39.3
Japan	19.8	21.0	34.3
Service			
Canada	37.0	44.7	60.9
United States	38.2	51.7	61.6
England	43.6	45.7	52.0
Germany	27.6	36.6	45.9
France	26.7	32.9	43.7
Japan	23.9	28.7	45.7

Source: Adapted from Joachim Singelmann, "The Sectoral Transformation of the Labor
Force in Seven Industrialized Countries, 1920-1970," *American Journal of Sociology* 83
(1978): 1229, table 2. Italy is omitted here because data are lacking for the 1970 period.

Class Structure

An alternative way to categorize the labor force is by classes. Classes are groups defined by their control or lack of control over various aspects of economic production, rather than by differences in types and levels of job skills (e.g., manual or nonmanual workers). The most familiar and often used concept of classes is that articulated by Karl Marx. In his conceptualization, classes (and their amount of power) are determined by their relationships to the means of production: capital, land, technology, equipment, and so on. The basic class distinction Marx made for modern capitalist countries is between the bourgeoisie, who own the means of production and thus have substantial control over economic production, and the preletariat, who own only their own labor power and must sell it to the bourgeoisie in return for the wages that allow them to make a living. Having sold their labor power, the proletariat lack any control over economic production, including the use of their own labor.

Drawing upon the work of Eric Olin Wright, Donald Black and John Myles have provided a classification scheme for the Canadian labor force by class position (see table 6). This depiction of the Canadian class structure, and comparisons with those of the United States and Sweden, is based on surveys of random samples of the labor force rather than on census data.

a) Class categories are defined as follows:

1. *Large employers* = Self-employed owners who employ ten or more other workers.
2. *Small employers* = Self-employed owners who employ fewer than ten other workers.
3. *Petit bourgeoisie* = Self-employed owners who employ no other workers.
4. *Managers* = Nonowners who participate in their company's policy-making decisions concerning the use of capital and labor power.
5. *Supervisors* = Nonowners who exercise authority over other employees.
6. *Semiautonomous employees* = Employees who retain some control over how they do their own work and what they produce.
7. *Workers* (proletariat) = Employees who have no authority over others and no control over their own work or what they produce.

18

Table 6

Class Structures of Canada, the United States, and Sweden

Class Category[a]	Percentage of Population		
	Canada	United States	Sweden
Large employers	0.9%	1.8%	0.7%
Small employers	2.8	6.0	4.7
Petit bourgeoisie	12.3	6.8	5.3
Managers	14.6	17.1	14.7
Supervisors	10.0	12.7	7.0
Semiautonomous employees	16.0	9.4	16.8
Worker (proletariat)	43.4	46.0	50.9
Total	100.0%	100.0%	100.0%
N	(1,756)	(1,415)	(1,133)

Source: Don Black and John Myles, "Dependent Industrialization and the Canadian Class Structure: A Comparative Analysis of Canada, The United States and Sweden," *Canadian Review of Sociology and Anthropology* 23 (1986): 162, table 1.

Black and Myles note a number of features that distinguish the Canadian class structure from those of the other two countries, and they suggest that some of these distinctive features result from extensive American ownership in the Canadian economy. First, Canada has a smaller percentage of its labor force in either the top "employers" (bourgeoisie) or bottom (proletariat) class categories than does the United States or Sweden. Black and Myles point out that foreign-owned firms, or multinational corporations, tend to use highly automated production technologies that reduce their demand for local labor in the production process, thus resulting in a smaller percentage of "workers." Also, because of the large size and extensive resources available to multinationals, extensive foreign ownership reduces the ability of locally owned firms to compete directly, resulting in a smaller percentage of "employers." Thriving locally owned firms tend to be small and to be located in markets not dominated by the multinationals, such as farming or services. As a result, a relatively large percentage of Canadians are categorized as "petit bourgeoisie"—self-employed owners who do not employ other labor, such as small shopkeepers or family farmers. For Black and Myles, this argument helps explain the persistence of this group in Canada in contrast to other industrial countries where such groups have diminished in response to the tendencies of capitalistic economic development to increase the concentration of economic production in ever-larger firms.

Another feature of the Canadian class structure is worth noting. The percentage of semiautonomous workers in the Canadian labor force (workers who have maintained some control over their own work) is almost double that for the United States and close to the percentage for Sweden. Black and Myles attribute this difference to national differences in the organization of production activities. They argue that the United States has a distinctive pattern of organization that results in a strict division between administrative workers (managers and supervisors) and production workers. Workers are either incorporated into administration or stripped of their autonomy. Thus, very few with autonomy are not part of management. Although Black and Myles do not provide reasons for these differences in organization, one possibility has to do with differences in the strength of labor unions. Whereas only 18 percent of nonagricultural workers in the United States belonged to labor unions as of 1985, 40 percent of nonagricultural Canadian workers belonged. Because one goal of unions is to obtain, or at least maintain, some control over the production process by their members, through mechanisms like work rules, it could be argued that the extent to which this goal may be attained is positively related to the proportion of workers who are unionized—thus the greater the percentage of semiautonomous Canadian workers.

Education

Like other industrial democracies, in particular the United States, Canada has experienced a dramatic increase in the overall level of education of its population since World War II. Indeed, the education revolution may have been even more dramatic in Canada than in the United States. According to the Organization for Economic Cooperation and Development, until the late 1940s, Canada was "one of the least educationally developed of the great democracies." However, by the 1980s, Canada ranked as one of the world's most educated countries. This change was compelled both by postwar baby boom and immigration-based population growth and by rising expectations concerning occupational opportunities and the belief in education as a means to obtain those opportunities. As a result, expenditures on education have risen from 2.4 percent of Canada's gross domestic product in 1950 to over 8 percent in 1991.

20

Nowhere has this education revolution been more apparent than at the post-secondary, or higher education level. Since World War II Canadian universities have expanded dramatically—both in number and size. Government funding led to the opening of many new universities, such as York in Toronto, Carleton in Ottawa, and the University of Quebec at Montreal. Similarly, the proportion of Canadians within the age group (ages twenty to twenty-four) normally attending colleges and universities in Canada rose from 16 percent in 1960 to 36 percent in 1979, a 125 percent increase. However, although the rate of enrollment growth in Canadian higher education compares favorably with that of the United States (72 percent over the same time period), Canada continues to lag considerably behind its neighbor in actual proportions enrolled. In the United States in 1960, 32 percent of persons between the ages of twenty and twenty-four were enrolled in institutions of higher education, and that figure had increased to 55 percent by 1979.

Income

Canada, like the United States, is one of the most affluent countries in the world. In fact, median Canadian and U.S. family incomes in the early 1990s were virtually indentical—approaching US $36,000 (see table 7). In "constant dollars" (i.e., controlling for inflation) Canadian as well as Americans median incomes have doubled since the late 1940s, but most of these gains were made before the early 1970s. Since then, real income has not increased substantially in either country, and during the 1980s and early 1990s real income actually eroded somewhat. These most recent trends are seen as the result of the movement of many manufacturing industries out of North America and the movement of the North American labor force into less well paying jobs in service industries.

The overall income distributions in the United States and Canada also are similar, except at the bottom. Both countries have a sizable group of middle-income families, but even taking into account the differing values of the Canadian and U.S. dollars, considerably fewer Canadian families are at the bottom of the income distribution. This situation could indicate more rapid transition to a service-dominated economy in the United States than in Canada or substantial reductions in social welfare supplements to low-income families in the United States. Regardless, the percentages of low-income families in both Canada and the United States increased in the 1980s and 1990s over their levels of the 1970s.

The characteristics that are the most important determinants of income also are similar in Canada and the United States. In both countries, income is largely a function of the level of education, occupation, class, and industry. The highest

21

Table 7

Distribution of Family Income in Canada and the United States, 1991

Canada (1991)	Family Income[a]	United States (1991)	Family Income[b]
Under CDN$10,000	2.4	Under US$10,000	9.7%
CDN$10,000-CDN$29,999	24.1	US$10,000-US$24,999	23.3
CDN$30,000-CDN$49,999	27.6	US$25,000-US$49,999	35.1
CDN$50,000-CDN$74,999	26.2	US$50,000-US$74,999	18.8
CDN$75,000 +	19.6	US$75,000+	13.1
Total	99.9%[c]		100.0%[c]
Median income	CDN$46,742[d]		US$35,939[d]

a. From Statistics Canada, *Canada Year Book 1994* (Ottawa: Ministry of Supply and Services Canada), 216, table 6.17.
b. From U.S. Bureau of Census, *Money Income of Households, Families, and Persons in the United States: 1991*. Current Population Reports, Series P.60, No. 180 (Washington, D.C.: U.S. Government Printing Office, 1992), 44, table 14.
c. Deviation from 100 percent because of rounding.
d. The Canadian dollar was worth approximately 70 to 75 percent of the U.S. dollar in international exchange.

incomes go to college graduates, professionals, employers (owners, or bourgeoisie) and workers in industries that operate in oligopolistic markets—that is, markets dominated by a very few firms, so that prices and workers' wages are not determined directly by competitive market pressures (petroleum, auto, steel, public administration, banking, etc.). In addition, ascriptive characteristics, such as gender and ethnicity, are important determinants of income. In both countries men earn more than women, and whites in the United States and English-speaking Canadians earn the most. Indeed it is this last difference that has been the source of some of the most bitter and enduring conflicts in both countries, a point that is addressed in the next section.

Summary

This profile of Canada's demographic and socioeconomic characteristics has highlighted several points. First, Canada's general profile is similar to that of certain other industrial countries. Like the United States and Australia, countries with which Canada is often compared, Canada has benefited from its history as a white-settler, frontier nation, as well as from its geography as a continent-spanning nation. Second, Canada's small population-to-land ratio has maintained high wage levels for its labor force, encouraged technological innovation within industry to compensate for labor costs and labor shortages, and has meant that Canada has not had to face severe overcrowding or devastating depletion of its vast natural resources. Nor is overcrowding or depletion of resources likely to occur in the foreseeable future. Because so much of Canada's population growth results from immigration, it is growth that can be controlled. Third, Canada has not escaped the problems of other industrial societies—aging, health care costs, crime, deindustrialization, and poverty, but, its policies for addressing these problems are different from those of other nations. Canada's public sector is more involved in many of these issues, like health care, than in the case of the United States, but less involved than in many European countries, such as Sweden and Britain. And, finally, Canada's unique history and geography have caused the country's two most difficult problems, lack of cohesion and identity, which are discussed in the sections that follow.

The Issue of Cohesion: Cultural and Regional Diversity

In this section, we consider the issue of cohesion, or integration, among cultural groups and regions within Canada. We begin by looking at the extent of ethnic, linguistic, and religious diversity that exists in the country. Then we discuss the most enduring aspect of that diversity, the conflict between French and English Canada. The focus is on the various causes of that conflict along with its most recent manifestation, the Quebec separatist movement. Finally, we examine regional inequalities and conflicts within English Canada, as well as their economic and political outcomes.

Ethnic and Linguistic Diversity

The particular ethnic mix of Canadian society has changed over the years as the origins of Canada's immigrants have changed. From Jacques Cartier's landing at what is now Quebec City in the sixteenth century until the British conquest of 1759, almost all immigrants came from France. From 1759 until the early twentieth century the largest numbers came from the British Isles. During this

Table 8.
Canada's Population by Selected Ethnic Origins, 1981
(Percentage)

Ethnic Origin	CDA	NFLD	PEI	NS	NB	QUE	ON	MAN	SASK	ALTA	BC	YT	NWT
British	43.5%	94.9%	82.9%	79.3%	56.8%	7.8%	57.9%	41.0%	42.9%	49.6%	57.5%	51.4%	24.2%
French	28.9	2.8	13.1	9.3	38.7	81.8	8.4	8.1	5.5	5.8	3.8	5.5	4.2
Other	27.6	2.3	4.0	11.4	4.5	10.4	33.7	50.9	51.6	44.6	38.7	43.1	71.6
Total	100.0	100.0	100.0	100.0	100.0	100.0	100.0	100.0	100.0	100.0	100.0	100.0	100.0

Note: These figures include the percentage of population with single ethnic origins only. Persons with multiple ethnic origins account for 7.6 percent or the Canadian population.

Source: Adapted from Statistics Canada, *Canada Yearbook 1985*, 60, table 2.20.

a. British origins include all persons with origins from the British Isles: England, Scotland, Ireland, and Wales.

Abbreviations: CDA Canada

NFLD-Newfoundland	MAN-Manitoba
PEI-Prince Edward Island	SASK-Saskatchewan
NS-Nova Scotia	ALTA-Alberta
NB-New Brunswick	BC-British Columbia
QUE-Quebec	YT-Yukon Territory
ON-Ontario	NWT-Northwest Territories

century, immigrants have increasingly come from southern and eastern Europe and from non-European countries.

Today, Canada's ethnic makeup reflects these shifts in immigration, although the two largest ethnic groups continue to be British (43.5 percent) and French (28.9 percent) (see table 8.) Among the quarter-plus of Canada's population that has neither British nor French origins, the largest ethnic groups are German (4.7 percent), Italian (3.1 percent), Ukrainian (2.2 percent), Dutch (1.7 percent), and native peoples—Canadian Indians and Inuit (1.7 percent).

Canada's ethnic groups tend to be geographically concentrated. Although outside Quebec the most common ethnic group is British, the dominance of this group ranges from 95 percent of Newfoundland's population to 24 percent of the Northwest Territories. In Quebec, French outnumber British by more than ten to one, but outside Quebec and neighboring New Brunswick, French ethnicity is no longer very common. In fact, the percentage of French Canadians is lower than the percentage of German Canadians in every province west of Ontario. Another way to demonstrate the concentration of French ethnicity in Quebec is to point out that 79 percent of all Canadians of French origin live in that province.

Canada's ethnic makeup is often described as a "mosaic," to contrast with the "melting pot" metaphor used to describe ethnic relations in the United States. The *melting pot* ideally characterizes a process by which diverse cultural groups lose their original identity as they assimilate (or blend) into a new American culture; *mosaic* recognizes the maintenance of diverse cultural identities that are pieced together to make a whole (Canadian culture). Whereas American public policy historically has encouraged and even forced assimilation, Canadian public policy has encouraged the maintenance of this mosaic through programs and grants that support the promotion and preservation of Canada's diverse cultural heritages.

This policy of multiculturalism has evolved from the realities of Canadian social development: because of the vastness of Canada's territory, cultural groups have often been able to live in separate communities isolated from contact with other cultural groups.

Canada is officially a bilingual nation, which means that French and English have equal standing in federal law. Canadians are encouraged, at least by the federal government, to become fluent in both languages. The dimension of language use—French, English, or both (bilingual)—complicates and exacerbates the basic division in ethnic identity between English and French Canadians. Although language use is closely related to ethnic identity, the two do not coincide exactly. Moreover, the differences between Canadians' language use and their ethnic identity are systematic, as can be best understood through examination of table 9.

Table 9

Canada's Population by Mother Tongue and Official Language, 1981

A. *Mother Tongue*

Province or Territory	English	French	Other	Total
Newfoundland	98.7%	.5%	.8%	100.0%
Prince Edward Island	93.9	5.0	1.1	100.0%
Nova Scotia	93.6	4.3	2.1	100.0%
New Brunswick	65.1	33.6	1.3	100.0%
Quebec	11.0	82.4	6.6	100.0%
Ontario	77.4	5.5	17.1	100.0%
Manitoba	71.7	5.1	23.2	100.0%
Saskatchewan	79.6	2.6	27.8	100.0%
Alberta	80.9	2.7	26.4	100.0%
British Columbia	82.0	1.7	26.3	100.0%
Yukon	87.4	2.5	10.1	100.0%
Northwest Territories	54.1	2.7	43.2	100.0%
Canada	61.3%	25.7%	13.0%	100.0%

B. *Fluency in Official Language*

Province or Territory	English	French	English or French	Neither	Total
Newfoundland	97.6%	0.0%	2.3%	0.1%	100.0%
Prince Edward Island	91.7	0.2	8.1	0.0	100.0%
Nova Scotia	92.3	0.2	7.4	0.1	100.0%
New Brunswick	60.5	13.0	26.5	0.1	100.0%
Quebec	6.7	60.1	32.4	0.8	100.0%
Ontario	86.7	0.7	10.8	1.7	100.0%
Manitoba	90.3	0.3	7.9	1.5	100.0%
Saskatchewan	94.6	0.1	4.6	0.8	100.0%
Alberta	92.4	0.2	6.4	1.0	100.0%
British Columbia	92.8	0.1	5.7	1.4	100.0%
Yukon	91.9	0.0	7.9	0.2	100.0%
Northwest Territories	79.9	0.1	6.0	1.2	100.0%
Canada	67.0%	16.6%	15.3%	1.2%	100.0%

Source: Adapted from Statistics Canada, *Canada Yearbook 1985*, 58-59, tables 2.18 and 2.19.

The table contains two measures of language group affiliation in the 1981 census: Panel A measures mother tongue, the primary language used by parents in the house where the respondents were reared, while Panel B measures fluency in the official languages. Two important facts concerning language group relations emerge. First, as with ethnic identity, language groups are concentrated geographically. English is the dominant language outside Quebec, and French is concentrated in Quebec and declines as one moves farther from that province. In every province west of Quebec the percentage of the population with French mother tongue is smaller than the percentage with "other" (non-English, non-French) mother tongue. Second, the figures indicate a process of assimilation of non-British ethnic groups, including French, to the English language. For every province, including Quebec, the percentage of persons with English mother tongue is higher than the percentage of those with British ethnic identity, as reported in table 8. In contrast, the percentage reporting "other" mother tongue is smaller in every province than the percentage reporting "other" (non-French, non-English) ethnic identity. And outside Quebec, the percentage with French mother tongue is smaller than the percentage with French ethnic identity. In other words, except for the French in Quebec, non-British Canadians are growing up in homes where English is the main language.

Comparison of panels A and B of table 9 suggests that the assimilation process is proceeding one more step. In every province except Quebec and New Brunswick, the percentage fluent in the English language is greater than the percentage of the population with English mother tongue. This means that even those Canadians not reared by English-speaking parents are learning English as their primary language. This is true even for the French outside Quebec and New Brunswick. For example, in Ontario where more than 8 percent of the population has French ethnic identity, only 5.5 percent come from homes where French was the primary language, and less than 1 percent are fluent in only their native language. And even where there are large concentrations of French, as in Quebec and New Brunswick, there is evidence that these people are becoming fluent in English as well as French. Such bilingualism is not apparent among those with English or "other" mother tongues outside Quebec and New Brunswick.

Language assimilation largely reflects the reality of living and working in English-speaking North America, but assimilation does not work in reverse. In Quebec, where French is dominant, non-French people are not becoming unilingual francophones; as with the French in the province, they appear to be becoming more bilingual. As a response to this trend, the Quebec National Assembly passed legislation in 1977 designed to preserve and foster the French language.

Bill 101 effectively made Quebec a unilingual French province by restricting most public and business uses of English. This legislation was provoked by fears among French Quebecers that assimilation to English was occurring even where French was the dominant language, and that, if left unchecked, French would become a minority language even in Quebec.

Of those Canadians speaking neither French nor English (table 9, panel B), the largest groups are native peoples—both the Canadian Indians and Inuit. As pointed out earlier, together these groups make up less than 2 percent of Canada's population. Indian groups are largely concentrated in Ontario and the three prairie provinces, where substantial numbers live on reservations. The greatest concentrations of Inuit are in northern Quebec, as well as the Northwest Territories, where they are the largest ethnic group. Almost all Inuit speak the Inukitut language; among native Indians there is much greater linguistic diversity, with over fifty Indian dialects belonging to ten major linguistic groups.

Another significant aspect of Canadian cultural identity concerns religion. Most Canadians, like most Americans, are Christians, but unlike the religious distribution in the United States, Canadians belonging to the Roman Catholic church outnumber those belonging to all Protestant denominations combined. According to the 1991 census, 45.7 percent of Canadians are Roman Catholic, while 36.3 percent belong to Protestant denominations, the largest being the United Church of Canada (15.6 percent) and Anglican (10.1 percent). No other Protestant denominations accounted for more than 5 percent of the population. Among other religions, about 3 percent of Canadians belong to either Greek or Eastern orthodox churches; slightly over 1 percent are Jewish; about the same number belong to Eastern, non-Christian faiths; and more than 7 percent claimed no religious preference.

Religious preferences are closely tied to ethnic identity and language group. Almost all French Canadians are Catholic, while the majority of English-speaking Canadians are Protestant. This also means that religious affiliations, like ethnicity and language, are geographically concentrated. All provinces except Quebec and New Brunswick have a Protestant majority, and nearly half of all Catholics (49 percent) live in Quebec.

The collection of these statistics in the Canadian census underscores the importance of cultural diversity to the Canadian government. Unlike the U.S. census, the Canadian census insists that people identify themselves by their non-Canadian ethnic origins (the U.S. census does this for race and for certain Hispanic and Asian origins). The Canadian classification by religious prefer-ences is also different from the U.S. census, which is prohibited from collecting this information because of the constitutional separation of church and state. In contrast, religion is publicly recognized in Canada, and although there is no official state religion, church-sponsored activities, like parochial schools, often receive public financial support.

The public nature of religion in Canada goes back to its original British and French settlements. In contrast to many of the early settlements in what became the United States, early colonists in Canada were not dissenters but people who wanted to retain ties to their mother country through the state, commerce, and religion. This was especially true in Quebec. Moreover, the British conquest of Quebec actually strengthened church-state ties. In exchange for support for British rule (and opposition to the revolt in the thirteen lower colonies), the British turned over administration of Quebec to the Catholic church, an agreement that was formalized in the Quebec Act of 1774. The church thus became the dominant institution in the province, a position it maintained until the 1960s. The greatest concern for the church and for most French Quebecers was "survival"—maintaining a French-speaking, Catholic culture in the midst of the overwhelmingly English-speaking and Protestant environment of North America. But social changes within and outside Quebec have reduced the power of the Catholic church in that province and secularized the language conflict, as the next section shows.

Quebec and French-English Conflict

From "Survival" to "Flowering"

From the Quebec Act into the twentieth century, survival of the French culture in Quebec was maintained through its isolation from anglophone society in church-dominated rural communities. These French communities were able to maintain their cultural strength and cohesiveness through the leadership of ultra-conservative priests, many of whom had fled France in opposition to the liberalizing effects of the French Revolution; these priests exercised tight control over the French population through the church's parish system and parochial education. They were aided in their efforts by an extremely high birthrate ("revenge of the cradle"). (In fact, the communities became overpopulated; as a result, there was massive emigration to the industrial New England states.) This "defensive" nationalism was also reflected in a conservative provincial government that did not interfere with anglophone control over Quebec's economic development. And because anglophone interests were concerned primarily with economic development, they reciprocated by not interfering in French culture—at least not in Quebec.

29

To be sure, not all French Canadians were happy with this arrangement. Despite periodic conflicts, however, anglophone dominance of Quebec's economy went unchallenged as long as francophones remained isolated in their rural communities, but by the early twentieth century this isolation was ending. Industrialization, along with overpopulation of French rural communities, led to increasing francophone migration to urban areas, especially Montreal, in search of work. In turn, urbanization led to increased competition with anglophones for jobs in businesses that were owned and controlled by anglophones, and in which English was the language of work. Outside Quebec, where francophones were in the minority, these social changes resulted in their assimilation to English. In Quebec, however, where francophones were the majority, these changes led not to assimilation, but to an increased sense of group awareness and relative deprivation. Moreover, these feelings were intensified by the erosion of traditional French Canadian culture and institutions, especially the church. With urbanization, the church could not exercise the tight controls that it could in small rural communities. The French Canadian birthrate declined dramatically, and the French Canadians increasingly desired an education oriented toward improving their position in the industrial and technocratic economy rather than preserving traditional French Catholic values.

These changes culminated in 1960 with the beginning of the "Quiet Revolution." The initial goal of the Quiet Revolution was *rattrapage* ("catching up"), or modernizing Quebec society in order to bring it into the mainstream of North American economic development. The unstated goal was to obtain a large share of Quebec's economic growth for French Quebeckers. It also meant a more active role for the provincial government in Quebec's economy.

As the Quiet Revolution proceeded into the 1970s, Quebec's defensive cultural nationalism gave way to a more confident, assertive identity, symbolized by the replacement of the label *French Canadian* with *Québécois*. However, this *epanouissement* ("flowering") was accompanied by increasing disappointment and impatience with the pace of economic and social reforms, and growing concern about the viability of Quebecois culture within the existing structure of Canadian confederation. In addition, the continuing decline in francophone birthrates, increasing bilingualism, and increasing immigration of non-francophones to Quebec raised concerns that francophones would become a minority in the province in the not too distant future.

The combination of an increasingly assertive cultural identity and growing concerns about the future of that identity culminated in the election of the separatist Parti Quebecois (P.Q.) to the provincial government in 1976. This election

30

represented the symbolic climax of the changes Francophone Quebec society had undergone during the twentieth century. The provincial government had established itself as the institution through which quebecois culture would be maintained and advanced. It had become to the new Quebec what the church had been to the old Quebec.

The election of the P.Q. itself was not a mandate for separation. The party had run on issues of economic reform and charges of corruption in the incumbent Liberal government, and had made it clear that the issue of separatism would be decided by popular vote at a later date. That day came on 20 May 1980, when Quebec held a referendum. Quebecers were asked if they would give the P.Q. a mandate to negotiate a new agreement with the rest of Canada: "sovereignty-association," or a political independence accompanied by continued economic association with the rest of Canada. However, after a bitter campaign and intense opposition from the federal government, Quebec's electorate defeated the proposal by a margin of approximately three to two.

A number of reasons have been offered for the ultimate failure of the separatist movement and the defeat of sovereignty-association. Although increasing economic contacts with Anglophone fueled Quebecois nationalism, these contacts also limited how far that nationalism would go. Economic development not only increased ethnic competition but also increasingly integrated Quebec into the Canadian and North American economies. In turn, this integration increased the potential costs to Quebec of separation: loss of jobs and industry and the closing of Canadian markets to Quebec's products. Among those who perceived the greatest costs of separation, and thus who came to oppose sovereignty association, were French Canadian groups who had the strongest economic ties to anglophones. Paradoxically, these groups included business owners as well as segments of the new middle class that originally had supported the Quiet Revolution—professionals and managers in the private sector. Conversely, groups with the weakest ties were among those who most favored sovereignty-association. These groups included the "intellectual" elements of the new middle class, that is, teachers (especially college and university), journalists, and artists. P.Q. language legislation may have also helped defeat sovereignty-association. By making French the official language of the province in 1977, the P.Q. reduced fears about the future of the French language in Quebec, thus undermining the proseparatist argument that French language and culture could not be guaranteed within the existing Canadian Confederation.

The issue of separatism appeard to wane somewhat after the 1980 referendum. In 1985 the P.Q. was defeated and the Liberals returned to office. However,

31

a series of events over the next decade set the stage for its resurgence in the 1990s.

In 1982, the federal government and all provinces except Quebec agreed to a new indigenous ("patriated") Constitution to replace the 1867 British North American Act as Canada's legal foundation. Although legally bound by the new constitution the Quebec government refused to sign the document. It argued that the new Constitution failed to recognize Quebec's "special status" as the only French language province. To many francophone Quebeckers the need for such special status to protect their language was demonstrated in 1988 when the Canadian Supreme Court overturned Bill 101 because it violated the new constitution's guarantees of minority language rights (in this case, the rights of Anglophone and Allophone Quebeckers). However, Quebec's National Assmebly used another of the new constitution's provisions—the "notwithstanding" clause—to override the Supreme Court's decision and reestablished the primacy of the French language by passing Bill 178. The "notwithstanding" clause gives provincial legislatures the right to override court decisions inconsistent with provincial interests by exempting potentially offending legislation from court review for a limited time (five years).

During this same period, efforts were being undertaken by the federal and provincial governments to negotiate constitutional reforms that would give some recognition to Quebec's "special status" as a" distinct society" within Canada. Negotiations resulted in the 1987 Meech Lake Accord. When this Accord fell through in 1990 because the provincial legistlautes of Manitoba and Newfoundland failed to ratify it, a second round of negotiations resulted in the 1992 Charlottetown Accord. However, this Accord likewise fell through when voters in six provinces—including Quebec—voted against it in a special referendum in the fall of 1992. The overall effect of a decade of failed constitutional reform was to increase bad feelings between the francophone population of Quebec and the rest of Canada. Many Quebecers felt "humiliated" and "rejected" by non-French Canada, while many Canadians outside Quebec felt "angry" and "unsympathetic" toward what they considered endless demands for special privileges by Quebec.

At the same time, many Quebecers felt increasingly confident that the province could make it on its own economically. These feelings were fed by the growth of French-owned private sector businesses during the 1980s, and enhanced by the signing of the United States-Canada Free Trade Agreement (1988) and the North American Free Trade Act (1993). By eliminating tariffs on exports to the United States and Mexico, these trade agreements gave Quebec the opportunity of reorienting its trade from the rest of Canda to markets south of its border. Thus, many Quebecers saw the potential of reducing their economic dependence on Canada, and with it the costs of separation. As if a culmination of these events, the P.Q. was returned to power in 1994. It promised a second referendum on some form of separation to be held in 1995. However, opinion polls suggested that, despite unhappiness with constitutional reform efforts, a majority of Quebecers were opposed to separation.

Regional Conflicts within English Canada

Regional Economic Inequality

The other source of concern over the cohesiveness of Canadian society lies in the history of regional conflicts within English Canada. These conflicts are primarily the result of regional inequalities arising from differences in economic activities and resources. Central Canada, and especially Ontario, has always been the core of the Canadian economy, and thus has been historically the wealthiest region in Canada. Ontario became industrialized early and has maintained a more diversified economic base than the other provinces. In addition, most of the large Canadian financial and industrial corporations have headquarters in Ontario, and branch operations of many non-Canadian multinational enterprises are also located there. The other predominantly Anglophone provinces have been more specialized in their economic activities—especially in the extraction and selling of raw materials. The Atlantic provinces have specialized in agriculture and energy resources.

Quebec, as suggested earlier, is a different case. Although it has specialized more than Ontario in the production of nondurable industrial goods such as textiles and paper, its economic base more closely resembles the diversification of Ontario than the specialization of the other provinces.

This overspecialization in primary staple and extractive economic activities by Atlantic and western Canada accounts for much of the regional inequality within English Canada. Overspecialization of a peripheral hinterland combined with economic diversification of an industrialized core region results in increased "dependence" of the periphery on the economic resources and decisions of the core. Dependency is tied to the particular trading pattern in which the periphery sells its raw materials to the core and buys from the core more expensive manufactured and consumer goods. This trading leads to an outflow of economic resources, such as workers or capital for investment, from the periphery to the core. In turn, this outflow reduces the ability of the periphery to

33

diversify its economy by building up its own industrial base, while it increases the available resources in the core for further economic expansion. The outcome is ever-increasing inequality between core and periphery.

In addition, decisions made about economic activities in the periphery are made in the core. When industrialization does occur in the periphery, it is controlled by businesses located in the core. In times of economic growth, core firms expand their operations into peripheral regions to take advantage of their cheaper production costs (e.g., lower labor costs) and expanding consumer markets. In times of economic recession, however, these peripheral operations are the first to be cut back.

Government policies also can help create or alleviate regional inequality. In this regard, Canadian public policy can be viewed as historically inconsistent; sometimes increasing, sometimes decreasing regional inequalities. Many observers argue that the creation of an economic periphery, especially in western Canada, was a deliberate result of the formulation of the "National Policy" in the middle of the nineteenth century. This policy was, in part, a response to the loss of American and British markets for Canadian industrial goods, as a result of changes in the trading policies of Canada's two major trading partners. It was hoped that these markets could be replaced by an internal market for manufactured goods that would be created by unifying the colonies of British North America into the Canadian Confederation and settling the West with immigrants arriving from Europe. In addition, western agriculture would provide cheap food for consumer markets in central Canada and increase national income through export to foreign markets.

According to sociologist Harry Hiller, author of *Canadian Society: A Macro Analysis*, the most prominent symbol of western Canada's peripheral status was "discriminatory" rail freight rates, known as the "Crow rates," for the Crow's Nest Pass Agreement of 1897. In that agreement, the federal government approved the movement of grain west to east by railroad below cost in order to help western farmers get their produce to central Canadian markets. But because these low rates applied only to western agricultural products, they discouraged shipment of nonagricultural goods and thus retarded industrialization of the region. Furthermore, to compensate for the low agricultural rates, higher rates were charged for shipping manufactured goods west. And, because of the high protective tariffs of the National Policy, westerners had little choice but to buy these goods. Overall, the Crow rates helped maintain the West as a source of cheap agricultural goods, which they subsidized, as well as a market for expensive central Canadian manufactured goods. The rates were eliminated in 1983, this action may be symbolic of changing regional economics in Canada.

Indeed, recognition of the extent of regional inequality has led both federal and provincial governments to formulate policies designed to overcome regional disparities. Since the Depression of the 1930s, the federal government had addressed regional inequality through such policies as equalization payments to the poorer provinces and to their residents (tax revenues collected in wealthier provinces have been redistributed to pay for programs in poorer provinces) and investment credits to businesses that locate in poor regions. Critics point out that these programs have had limited effectiveness in encouraging economic development in peripheral provinces because, for example, these provinces purchase so many goods from Ontario that much of the money they receive from federal programs is diverted back to central Canada.

Under current policy the federal government lacks control over how provinces spend the various payments they receive from Ottawa. This situation has helped provincial governments formulate and execute thir own economic development programs. But because these programs are designed to meet what each province sees as its own particular development needs, they vary substantially from province to province, especially with respect to whether the private or public sector plays the leading role in development.

Recently, regional inequality in Canada, as measured by economic productivity and by individual income, appears to have declined. Thanks in large part to the energy boom of the 1970s, this trend toward regional convergence is most apparent in the western provinces, especially in Alberta. As shown in table 10, Alberta had moved above the national averages on important indicators of economic development. By 1977, its per capita productivity was 134 percent of the national average, as measured by its gross domestic product, making it the wealthiest province in this respect. By contrast, British Columbia and Ontario, the next most productive provinces, had GDPs equivalent to 111 percent and 110 percent of the national average, respectively. At the same time, Alberta's per capita income was 104 percent of the national average, ranking it below British Columbia (110 percent) and Ontario (109 percent).

The noticeable gap between Alberta's wealth as measured by per capita productivity (134 percent) and per capita income (104 percent) may be due to the laissez faire nature of its development policies. Such policies have allowed private industry to retain a greater share of wealth generated from energy production, rather than encouraging redistribution of this wealth throughout the population. Alberta has also failed to diversify its economy to the extent of provinces like British Columbia or Ontario. One result is that Alberta has a lower

Table 10

Changes in Provincial Economic Productivity and Personal Income in
Canada, 1970-1977

Province	Provincial Productivity per capita as % of National per capita productivity		Personal Income per Capita as % of National Average	
	1970	1977	1970	1977
Newfoundland	55.9%	52.9%	63.4%	68.1%
Prince Edward Island	53.3	50.5	66.6	67.2
Nova Scotia	69.9	66.6	77.5	79.5
New Brunswick	64.2	63.5	72.1	75.0
Quebec	90.2	87.8	88.8	93.2
Ontario	118.1	109.7	118.6	109.5
Manitoba	90.8	91.4	93.0	93.2
Saskatchewan	78.4	96.5	72.5	92.2
Alberta	108.4	134.1	99.4	104.5
British Columbia	106.0	111.1	108.6	109.9
Canada	100.0	100.0	100.0	100.0

Source: From Judith Maxwell and Caroline Pesticau, *Economic Realities of Contemporary Confederation* (Montreal: C.D. Howe Research Institute, 1980), 70-71. The figures are based on statistics collected originally by Statistics Canada.

percentage of highly paid professionals in its labor force, a fact that helps account for the lag in per capita income behind British Columbia and Ontario.

In contrast to the West, the Atlantic provinces continue to lag far behind in both productivity and individual income. Unlike the West, these provinces lack natural resources that fetch high prices on world markets. As shown in table 10, Newfoundland and Prince Edward Island have per capita productivity that is barely half the national average. Nova Scotia and New Brunswick do not fare much better. The fact that the per capita incomes of the Atlantic provinces are higher than their productivity is in part due to federal development policies, such as income equalization payments, which redistribute income to residents in these provinces.

The figures in table 10 also suggest that central Canada—Ontario and Quebec—were economically stagnant during the 1970s. Per capita productivity declined in both Ontario and Quebec; per capita income also declined in Ontario. Much of this stagnation was brought about by the rapid increases in energy prices during the 1970s. By forcing highly industrialized central Canada to pay more for its energy, western Canada, in effect, forced redistribution of economic wealth from central to western Canada. This redistribution parallels the economic shift from the Rust Belt areas of the American Midwest and Northeast to the Sun Belt areas of the South and West. However, as with this regional shift in the United States, the shift of wealth to western Canada did not result in a corresponding shift in economic power. The major economic institutions, and thus the major economic decisions, have remained in central Canada and abroad.

Regionalism and Politics

Regional conflict is also a consequence of the structure of the Canadian political system. As noted earlier, Canada is a decentralized confederation in which provincial governments retain a great deal of autonomy in social and economic policies. Therefore, provincial governments provide important institutional vehicles for the pursuit of local interests. In contrast, at the federal level, the parliamentary system contains features that inhibit the expression of local and regional interests; these features include the principle of "representation by population" in the House of Commons, which provides for greater representation for areas with larger populations. Because two-thirds of Canada's population live in Ontario and Quebec, it is possible for a party to win a federal election without winning a single parliamentary seat in any of the other eight provinces.

The most significant feature inhibiting regional expression, however, is the strong party discipline required in parliament. Because a party can form a government only so long as it obtains a majority vote on major legislation, party members are constrained to vote for government policies, whether the constituents in their own districts favor the policies or not. Reinforcing this discipline is the fact that, because parties play the major role in selecting and funding parliamentary candidates, members' careers depend more on their party and its success than on their local constituency.

This party discipline and unity do not extend to relations between party organizations at the federal and provincial levels. Because federal and provincial elections are held independent of each other and almost always at different times, party organizations at the two levels also are independent of one another. When combined with a lack of representation in the federal parliament, this organizational independence encourages provincial parties to act as representatives of provincial interests to the federal government, rather than as representatives of a national party in provincial governments. The result is that the most significant political conflicts are often not between two different parties at the same level of government, but between governing parties at the provincial and federal levels, even if they are the same party.

Regionalism also has significantly affected the structure of Canadian politics by giving rise to "third party" political movements, which challenge the two dominant national Canadian parties: the Liberals and the Progressive Conservatives. Like the Parti Quebecois, these third parties in English Canada have attempted to gain power by mobilizing support for regional (or provincial) interests and attacking domination of the local economy by outside political and economic institutions. Unlike the P.Q., however, they have not seriously proposed political separation as a solution to regional economic problems—except for a small separatist party in Alberta.

The discipline of parliamentary parties is also conducive to the rise of regional and nonregional third parties. Because of the unity required to govern, parliamentary parties are less able than American congressional parties to incorporate or co-opt dissident factions into their ranks. As a result, dissidents often feel that they have no choice but to form a separate, third party.

Of the many regional third parties that have emerged in Canada, the most famous and successful have been the Social Credit in Alberta in the 1930s and the Cooperative Commonwealth Federation (CCF) in Saskatchewan in the 1940s. Although these two third parties had similar themes of local exploitation by outside economic forces, the strategies they offered for ending that exploitation were dramatically different. Social Credit was (and remains) a right-wing party which, although critical of the domination of large financial institutions headquartered in central Canada, has nonetheless supported the basic economic principles of capitalism. In many ways it has represented the interests of small business against those of large corporations and big government. In contrast, the CCF (now the New Democratic party or NDP) has been a party in the tradition of European democratic socialism; it has sought basic changes in the capitalist structure of the Canadian economy through democratically achieved reforms rather than revolution.

Many observers argue that the success of such ideologically different political movements in neighboring provinces was the result of differences in the social organization of agriculture in the two provinces and to differences in political alliances maintained by agricultural producers. Although agriculturalists in both provinces produced commercially for eastern Canadian and international markets, there was an important difference in what they produced: wheat in

Saskatchewan and livestock (mostly beef) in Alberta. This difference is significant because livestock ranching involves little overhead (e.g., for equipment or storage) and thus low indebtedness; but it produces relatively high and stable profits. In contrast, wheat farming requires higher overhead costs and thus a high level of indebtedness; yet it has relatively low and highly unstable profit levels. The result is that ranchers enjoy greater economic security than farmers, a difference that leads to different political orientations. According to Robert Brym, who has analyzed the regional social structure and agrarian radicalism in Canada, because of their low overhead and lack of debt, ranchers tend to see themselves as "romantic, isolated entrepreneurs" engaged in individualistic operations. Conversely, high overhead and debt lead wheat farmers to engage in cooperative ventures; by pooling their resources in farming co-ops they can reduce their individual overhead and increase their market power. In turn, wheat farmers develop a more egalitarian, collectivist orientation. This orientation is one reason for the history of political alliances between agrarian radicals and labor parties in Saskatchewan prior to the rise of the CCF, an alliance that helped push Saskatchewan's wheat farmers to the left. No such rancher-worker alliance developed in Alberta.

No significant regional third parties have emerged in Canada's poorest region, the Atlantic provinces. Their absence is partly attributable to the organization of agriculture in this region. Unlike the vast, open, flat, fertile farmlands of the prairies, Atlantic Canada is characterized by rugged, hilly, forested, unfertile terrain. These characteristics reduced the potential for commercial agriculture and, instead, encouraged subsistence farming. In turn, subsistence farming did not require high overhead and indebtedness, nor did the livelihoods of subsistence farmers depend on the vagaries of distant markets and financial institutions. As a result, no strong feelings of exploitation by outsiders developed among Atlantic farmers.

The region's rugged terrain also increased the isolation of its farmers. Instead of living in farm communities, Atlantic farmers tend to live alone and apart, a practice further encouraged by the British regime's granting of large tracts of land to Loyalists fleeing the American Revolution to Atlantic Canada. This isolation significantly reduced the potential for the development of common interests and common political action among farmers in the region.

Regionalism is also expressed in routine Canadian politics. Support for federal political parties varies by region. The Liberals historically receive most of their support in central Canada—Ontario and Quebec, among both anglophones and francophones—but receive very little support in the West. The Progressive

Conservatives traditionally have been stronger in the West and Atlantic Canada, while the New Democratic party receives its support from Ontario and the West. Such differences not only reflect the history of regional conflicts, but also help maintain and reinforce regionalism.

Recently, regionally based parties have even elected a substantial number of members to the federal Parliament, at the expense of the Progressive Conservatives and New Democrats. After the 1993 federal elections which the Liberals won by gaining a majority of the seats,

the Bloc Quebecois—an avowedly separatist party—formed the "official opposition," i.e., held the second largest block of seats in Parliament (even though it ran exclusively in Quebec). The third largest party in Parliament was the western-based Reform, all of whose seats, except one in Ontario, were gained in western provinces.

However, unlike the Bloc Quebecois, Reform's goal was not western separation, but greater representation by western provinces in federal instituions. Most notably, it sought a federal Senate in which members were elected, not appointed, in which each province had an equal number of senators—like the U.S. Senate—and which had an effective vote on important legislation.

Summary

Regional and cultural conflicts are not unique to Canada. Most industrial societies have undergone periods of intense conflict. Nor is the persistence of these conflicts uniquely Canadian. One has only to look at the history of race relations in the United States and the continuing remanifestations of its regional conflicts—between North and South, East and West, or Rust Belt and Sun Belt—to appreciate the difficulties of resolving, once and for all, regional and cultural conflicts within industrial societies. However, the conflicts in Canada have some unique and contradictory aspects. Regional and cultural conflicts in Canada almost always bring into question whether Canada has a future as a nation. Episodes of conflict inevitably generate political demands for some form of "devolution" under wich some power of the federal government would be assigned to provincial or local governments and occasionally for "continentalism"' (closer economic and political ties with the United States).

Despite the periodic intensity of these conflicts in Canada and the radical nature of some of the demands for devolution and continentalism, the conflicts have been contained within an effectively functioning democratic political system. Political violence associated with these conflicts has been extremely rare in

Canada and has never been a systematic part of strategies used by the opposing sides—even in the case of the separatist movement in Quebec. This feature of Canadian society is rather remarkable when one looks at the amount of violence associated with cultural and regional conflicts in some other countries.

Recent events, such as the defeat of constitutional reforms designed to secure Quebec's place in Confederation, the victory of the P.Q. and its promise for a second referendum on Quebec separation, and the growing importance of regional parties in the federal Parliament, suggest a resurgnece of internal forces that have threatened the Canadian state and identity throughout its history. It is too early to say whether this new "crisis" will lead to devolution of the Canadian Confederation or give way to compromise and negotiated settlement like previous crises. Moreover, these internal forces do not appear to be the only threats to Canadian national identity. Many Canadians also see others threats, especially external ones, to that identity. This issue is addressed in the next section.

The Issue of Identity: Cultural and Institutional Forces

In this chapter we examine the extent to which Canada possesses a unique national identity and the origins of that identity. We look at the shared cultural values that go into making up this identity and the extent to which they provide a bridge across regional and linguistic divisions. In addition, we investigate the interrelationship between these values and Canadian institutional arrangements—especially political and economic—that also cut across the country's internal divisions. Finally, we examine the extent to which Canada's national identity and sovereignty are threatened by external forces: extensive foreign ownership of industry and the influences of the American media.

Canadian National Culture and Character

Linguistic and regional conflicts have raised questions not only about how cohesive the Canadian nation is, but also about whether Canadians have anything in common—such as national identity—that would give them a stake in the survival of their nation. Many observers argue that this identity, which could override regional and cultural divisions, is altogether lacking in Canada. Others see a weak national identity that is defined less in terms of what Canadian history or traditions are than in terms of what Canadians are not: Americans. The Canadian historian Frank Underhill once noted that Canadians are "the world's oldest and most continuing anti-Americans." This "negative" national identity is seen as resting on Canadians' concern about their nation's ability to survive the "ill-intentioned interventions and machinations of the United States."

Others have argued that, despite often defining itself in terms of what it is not, Canada has a set of values that constitute a uniquely Canadian identity, or "national character." The most influential discussion of these values is that of American sociologist Seymour Martin Lipset. Lipset sees American culture as the embodiment of the classic Enlightenment liberal, or Lockean, society, emphasizing egalitarian, individualistic, entrepreneurial, laissez-faire, antistatist, and universalistic achievement values. In contrast, Lipset says, Canadian culture tends toward traditional conservativism, or Toryism, emphasizing law-abiding, statist, particularistic, corporatist, merchantilist, and ascriptive values.

Lipset sees these value differences as arising from differences in historical experiences, most notably the American Revolution and the refusal of Canada to join in the Revolution. The Revolution provided the United States with an early and profound break with Britain and traditional European values. No such break occurred in Canada, which evolved slowly into an independent country.

The Canadian choice not to join the Revolution was made by the elites of both language groups who sought to defend their independence and identity by preserving traditional conservative values and rejecting the liberal values of both the American and French revolutions. As Lipset argues, English Canada exists because it rejected the principles of the Declaration of Independence. This rejection was aided by the emigration of British Loyalists from the rebelling colonies, a group that made up the backbone of English Canadian resistance to the Revolution and to later attempts by the United States to incorporate—or annex—Canada, as in the invasions of the War of 1812. Similarly, the conservative Catholic clerical elite in Quebec sought not only to protect French Catholic culture from the English Protestant culture of North America but also to isolate Quebec from the secular values embodied in the French Revolution.

The result of this rejection both predisposed Canadian culture toward traditional conservative values and denied that culture a founding mythology. The American Revolution was a self-conscious act of national birth; the ideology of the Revolution has provided an explanation for why the United States came into being and what it means to be an American, thus providing a strong national identity. In contrast, Canada had no indigenous founding ideology to justify independence and provide a sense of national purpose, save for the desire to "resist absorption into the American Republic."

A number of critics have taken Lipset's "national character" thesis to task. Hiller suggests that Lipset's emphasis on the value differences between Canadians and Americans is dated. Canadian sociologist Tom Truman argues that Lipset is also wrong in stating that Canada continues to be a more elitist and less egalitarian society.

Cultural Values and Canadian Institutions

The State and Public Policy

Lipset argues that Canadian values support greater government involvement in economic and social affairs than American values do in the United States. This is true not only for the Canadian left, but even more so for Canadian conservatives, especially in comparison with their counterparts in the states. Whereas American conservatives derive their values from the principles of the Revolution and laissez-faire economics, Lipset argues, Canadian conservatives derive their values from traditional European, or Tory, conservatism. This type of conservatism has its roots in the aristocratic principle of noblesse oblige—the obligation of the elites to take care of the needs of the masses. Tory conservatism emphasizes not only authority and hierarchy, but also benevolence and solidarity between elites and masses. Thus, it incorporates a collectivist or corporatist strain that is antithetical to the individualistic, antistatist orientation of American conservatism.

In contrast, Truman emphasizes the influence of the left in encouraging greater government involvement in Canada. He cites Canada's link to the British working class heritage through political communication and immigration. According to Truman, this heritage puts greater emphasis on equality of living standards and income, rather than competitive status attainment. This ideology has persisted in former British colonies in social democratic parties, such as the NDP, whose ranks have been filled by British working class immigrants.

Canada's history of a more activist central government was also reinforced by Canada's frontier expansion, which was quite different from the frontier expansion in the United States. Population movement in the United States occurred in response to natural demographic pressures such as cheap land and abundant opportunities. Because population movement ran ahead of the establishment of government authority (often intentionally so), autonomous frontier communities were often unprotected by sanctioned law enforcement organizations. As a result, law enforcement was in the hands of the settlers themselves. This type of frontier expansion also resulted in numerous Indian wars, as settlers intruded into Indian land, often in violation of Indian-U.S. government treaties.

Canada had a larger but less habitable frontier territory and a smaller population base; hence Canada had to be on guard against the expansionist tendencies of its neighbor. As a result, Canadian frontier development could not be autonomous or unprotected. Government authority had to operate well in advance of the spread of settlement. Frontier expansion had to be planned carefully rather than allowed to happen naturally. Such planning was furthered by the British tradition of centralized law enforcement. The primary response to this need for planned expansion was the establishment of the centrally controlled Northwest Mounted Police, which moved into the frontier ahead of and along with the settlers. Thus, Canadian frontier development lacked the vigilantism and Indian conflicts that characterized the U.S. frontier.

Greater deference to government authority is also seen in Canadian legal culture. Canadian law has operated on a "crime control model" typical of European countries. This model emphasizes the maintenance of law and order and the rights and obligations of the community over the rights of individuals and their protection from government intrusion that are emphasized in the American "due process model." As a result, the Canadian government has greater power to restrict individual freedoms than the U.S. government has. Moreover, government agencies have greater latitude to invade individual privacy and circumvent civil rights than agencies in the United States have. Laws are less restrictive of these covert activities, as apparently are public attitudes. For example, observers have contrasted the American public's outrage at the domestic spying activities of the CIA and FBI with the Canadian public's lack of concern with similar activities conducted systematically by the Royal Canadian Mounted Police during the 1970s.

Recently, however, Canada has been moving toward the due process model. This move culminated in 1982 with the adoption of the Charter of Rights and Freedoms to go along with the new constitution act. Much like the U.S. Bill of Rights, the charter creates a legal basis for judicial intervention to protect individual and civil rights. However, the charter allows for government to optout of these constitutional restrictions on its powers by inserting into any law a clause that the law will operate regardless of the charter. The charter thus guarantees parliamentary supremacy over the judiciary, a principle that stands in contrast to the U.S. principle of checks and balances among equal branches of government.

Differences between Canadian and U.S. legal cultures are also expressed in public attitudes and behavior. Canadians express in public opinion polls greater confidence in their police and support stronger punishment for criminals as well as for gun-control legislation. However, too much should not be made of these differences, because a majority of the public in each country supports law-and-order measures, such as longer prison sentences and tougher gun-control laws. In addition, as already indicated, Canadians are much less likely than Americans to commit violent crimes, like murder, robbery, and rape, or to be arrested for the use of illegal drugs. Finally, in support of this thesis, Lipset cites evidence that Canadians are much less likely to take part in political protest activities, such as riots and demonstrations.

The Canadian state also has a larger role in economic and social affairs, as evidenced by the larger portion of the GDP (44 percent) spent by government in Canada than in the United States (38 percent). If the higher levels of defense spending in the United States—about 6 percent of the GNP versus 2 percent in Canada is discounted, the gap is even wider. Another indicator of a larger role for government in Canada is taxes. As of 1982, taxes accounted for 35 percent of Canada's GDP versus 30 percent of the U.S. GNP. Because of this greater revenue, Canada is able to provide more public services, such as national health insurance, than does the United States. Canada also draws a less distinct line between public and private sectors, as is indicated by the large number of government-owned, or "Crown," corporations. These Crown corporations have not been the creations solely of left-of-center federal and provincial governments; conservative governments have often found it in their interest to establish these corporations as well.

There is considerably less hostility to such government activities in Canada than in the United States, as is evidenced by both public opinion surveys and the history of the development of government programs. Public opinion polls have consistently found Canadians less opposed to "big government" than Americans, and more likely to support the expansion of government-run social services, such as the provision of health care and a guaranteed minimum income. Moreover, the history of Canadian public policy has been characterized by a gradual, continuous process of program development in which opposition is minimized.

This situation contrasts with the American experience in which government programs are developed episodically in response to crises usually in the face of intense opposition. For example, the U.S. social security system was instituted in response to the Great Depression and has been reformed since only with great difficulty. This episodic history can be traced partly to the considerable opposition that government-funded social programs faced both from private interest groups and from people ideologically opposed to government initiatives, and partly to the division of authority between Congress and the president, which encourages stalemate in policy development. No comprehensive national program has yet been adopted in the United States, despite what many see as a health care and health insurance "crisis." Opposition from health care professionals, private insurance companies, and political conservatives remains intense.

In contrast, Canada took its first step toward social security during the relatively prosperous 1920s, and major structural reforms have been undertaken periodically including during prosperous times—1951 and 1965. These initiatives were aided by the unitary authority found in parliamentary governments. Similarly, Canada initiated its version of government-funded comprehensive national health care during the 1960s and early 1970s. Surprisingly, there was little opposition to this program from either health care professionals or conservatives.

In important ways Canada is a "consociational democracy"—a concept coined by the Dutch political scientist Arendt Lijphart to describe how accommodation was achieved in countries that were divided between culturally and geographically distinct groups, such as the Netherlands, Switzerland, and Canada. Lijphart's argues that the cleavages between these groups create such obstacles to accommodation that the public and most politicians grant the political "elites" wide-ranging discretion in the formation and implementation of public policy. In turn, the elites have an interest in maintaining the system of consociational democrary—and their position atop it—and are thus willing to compromise to develop policies that are workable and generally acceptable. Because policy stagnation is often an invitation to disunity, there is constant pressure on the system, and especially on the elites, for policy innovation. Thus, in Canada, responsibility for policy innovation rests with a few top cabinet ministers and civil servants at the federal and provincial levels. Federal-provincial conferences among these elites assume great importance in the accommodation process, both culturally and regionally. To minimize outside influence from interest groups, these conferences are closed to public and press and their proceedings are confidential except for a carefully worded and mutually agreed upon communique at their conclusion.

This consociational system of elite accommodations, in turn, works only because of the structure of the Canadian political system. For instance, accommodations between federal and provincial elites are facilitated by the facts that there are but ten provinces—not an unwieldy fifty—and that two provinces (Ontario and Quebec) contain most of the country's population. Also important is the unitary nature of political power in a parliamentary system. At both the federal and the provincial levels, the political executives—prime minister and premiers—have unrivaled (by legislative leaders) authority and can commit their governments to policies without much fear of being overruled. Moreover,

46

political parties in parliament need to maintain voting discipline to stay in power. In addition, a unique feature of Canadian history encourages policy innovation and accommodation: the election, from time to time, of minority governments at the federal level. Pressures for policy innovation are particularly great during minority governments when one of the dominant parties—Progressive Conservative or Liberal—must rely on the support of third parties to stay in power. Under these circumstances, the dominant parties are likely to adopt policy innovations put forth by third parties in exchange for their support on other issues, and to win over third-party voters so that they can achieve majority government status in the next election. For their part, third parties rely on dominant parties to implement their policy innovations. The development of social security and health insurance are both attributable in part to this kind of symbiotic relationship, in particular between the Liberal party and the CCF-NDP. And because most third parties have been regionally based, these interparty relations obviously aid the consociational accommodation process.

Economic Institutions and Practices

The character of Canadian national identity is also reflected in its economic institutions and values. Observers note a strain of traditional conservatism in explaining what they see as a lack of Canadian entrepreneurship: businesses are less aggressive, innovative, and willing to take risks than their U.S. counterparts. Canadian investors and financial institutions have been hesitant to provide venture capital, especially to newer, technologically based industries. Comparative studies have also found individual Canadians less willing to take risks than Americans. Investment is a much less significant source of income for Canadians, and they are less likely to rely on credit in purchasing consumer goods.

Many of these observers also see an elitist strain reflected in the patterns of social mobility in Canada. As mentioned earlier, in 1965, John Porter described Canada as a "vertical mosaic," in which ascriptive characteristics, particularly ethnicity, were more important than achieved characteristics, such as education, in determining occupational attainment. Porter largely blamed this hierarchical arrangement of ethnic groups on Canada's inadequate education system and values that did not promote mobility through free universal education. Historically, recruitment to elite positions in Canadian government and industry has been based more on class background than in the United States. One study conducted by Canadian sociologist Wallace Clement found that, during the 1970s, 61 percent of

Canadian top corporate executives were of upper-class background, i.e., came from families with substantial wealth and/or owned substantial capital property, compared with 36 percent of American top executives. Researchers also found a much higher proportion of Canadian than U.S. government bureaucrats to be from upper-class origins. Conversely, Canadian executives and bureaucrats were found to be less likely to have professional or technical education than their American counterparts. According to many observers, this recruitment pattern reflects an elitist, "generalist" approach to administration, closely patterned after the British administrative model, in which traditional authority is emphasized over authority based on technical expertise.

Evidence is growing that the old pattern of mobility is changing and that achievement criteria are becoming more important in Canada. As pointed out earlier, the number of Canadians attending higher education has dramatically increased in the past twenty years. In addition, many recent studies have found that Canada's overall rate of occupational mobility is not significantly lower than that for the United States (or any other industrial country), and that, as in the United States, educational attainment is the most significant determinant of occupational attainment.

Lipset has argued that the elitism and corporatism of Tory conservative values produce their antithesis in a leftist class consciousness among workers that is stronger than in societies with strong, individualistic, achievement values. Truman argues that this stronger class consciousness is a product of ties to the British working-class heritage. Both find evidence for this argument in the greater strength of Canadian socialist parties—CCF/NDP—and in the higher level of union membership in Canada than in the United States noted earlier. Moreover, union membership in Canada has doubled since the early 1950s, in contrast to a 50 percent decline in the United States over the same time. A major reason for the growth of Canadian unions has been the dramatic increase in membership among francophone Quebecers, a growth promoted in part by provincial governments since the Quiet Revolution as a way of countering anglophone economic power.

Despite this evidence of class consciousness among Canadian workers, class-based voting is very weak. The reason for this paradox most likely has to do with the fact that working-class parties, such as the NDP, often have been regionally based and thus did not contest elections in every parliamentary district in every province—Quebec or Atlantic Canada, for example. Thus, workers who might support such parties do not always have that opportunity. Where the NDP does compete, as in Manitoba or Ontario, the level of class voting is much greater.

As with its political system, Canada's economic system not only helps define a national identity distinct from the U.S. identity, but also cuts across regional and cultural boundaries—as well as reinforcing them at times. Economic authority in Canada is highly centralized. And, as with centralization of political authority, economic centralization is viewed as essential to maintain an integrated national economy by linking together regionally different production activities. Nowhere is this centralization greater than in the financial sector. In contrast to the United States, where banks are chartered by individual states, banks in Canada are chartered exclusively by the federal government. Hence banks operate nationally, rather than locally, there are few bank corporations, and the assets they control are highly concentrated (the financial market is oligopolistic). Between 1900 and 1972 the number of Canadian banks declined from thirty six to eleven. As of 1977, 90 percent of total bank assets were in the hands of the five largest banks, all of which rank among the fifty largest non-American corporations in the world.

These financial institutions are at the center of a dense network of interlocking directorates that integrates large-scale capital in Canada. One study found that of the 797 largest Canadian-owned firms, 724 were connected in a single interlocking network that cuts across both regions and potentially competitive groups of corporations, thus integrating capital on a national level. Research also shows that almost all these large firms are connected with at least one of the large Canadian banks. Canadian sociologists, John Fox and Michael Ornstein argue that these financial institutions serve as "articulating points" in this network, tying together the economic interests of industrial and financial firms.

Foreign Ownership and Economic Dependence

Canada is not unique in the centralization of economic authority or in the central role of its financial institutions in linking diverse corporate interests. Similar research in the U.S. and other industrial capitalist countries has arrived at similar results. But one feature of Canada's economic system distinguishes it from most other industrial nations: the large amount of foreign, especially U.S., ownership of its economic institutions. In this respect, Canada's economy is closer to those of many Third World countries than to those of the industrialized West. Many Canadians view this ownership as the single greatest threat to the country's national identity and even sovereignty.

By the mid-1970s, more than half of all assets in Canadian manufacturing (59 percent) and mining (56 percent) and more than three-quarters (76 percent) of all

49

assets in the Canadian petroleum and natural gas industry were controlled by for-eign-owned firms (i.e., firms with 50 percent or more non-Canadian ownership). American investment accounted for 77 percent of that total. Moreover, foreign ownership of certain industries was almost complete: 99 percent in rubber and 96 percent in automobile and parts manufacturing. Foreign investment is also reflected in the ownership of large firms doing business in Canada. In 1977, 29 of the 50 largest firms in Canada, and 135 of the top 200, were foreign-owned. There is no evidence that this foreign ownership has abated during the 1980s.

The role of foreign-owned firms in the Canadian economy has come under increasing criticism since the 1960s. Although there is little evidence that the extent of foreign ownership has reduced Canada's standard of living, as has often been the case with foreign ownership in Third World countries, there is some evidence that such ownership has at times retarded Canada's rate of economic growth. Critics argue that foreign-owned firms have distorted the Canadian economy in the direction of capital-intensive, resource extraction, while dimin-ishing development in manufacturing and high-technology industries. Furthermore, payment by Canadian branch plants to their foreign parent firms is viewed as a long-term drain of potential investment money out of the country. Finally, important decisions affecting virtually all sectors of the Canadian econ-omy are made outside the country, thus making the Canadian economy "pro-foundly dependent" on non-Canadian economic forces.

A number of theories have been proposed to account for Canada's particular form of economic dependency. The most prominent is "staples theory." According to the central argument of this theory, because of the country's long colonial status, Canada's economic elite, or capitalist class, has been dominated by a financial/commercial bourgeoisie whose economic interests are tied to profit making through the selling or trading of commodities, rather than their actual production. They have thus forgone making long-term fixed investments in manufacturing in favor of investing in the transportation and sale of staple products as exports. The results are underdevelopment of manufacturing indus-tries, reliance on imports of manufactured goods, and dependence on foreign export markets. According to staples theory, American branch plants have been established in Canada to fill the vacuum created by the lack of indigenous man-ufacturing industries.

Critics of this explanation of Canada's economic dependence argue that the staples theory does not account for the nineteenth-century industrialization that did occur, especially in Ontario. Nor, they argue, is the theory correct in drawing a distinction between financial and industrial capitalism—either in economic interests or often in actual persons. These critics believe that Canada's current economic dependence stems from the failure of early Canadian industry to develop the strength to keep foreign-owned industry out of the Canadian market, and from the disincentives for financial investments in Canadian industry. In an article on "Dependency and Class in Canadian Political Economy," Leo Panitch argues that these reasons, in turn, are related to the competitive disadvantage of early Canadian industry vis-a-vis American industry. He argues that this disadvantage derived from the high wage levels and militancy of nineteenth-century Canadian industrial workers which drove up production costs and thus squeezed profits, especially in the small Canadian market. In turn, high wages and militancy of Canadian workers were the result of the country's labor shortage, which forced industry to rely on a highly skilled work force. As a result, U.S. industry could underprice Canadian industries even in their own domestic markets, thus stunting the development of Canadian industry and making Canadian markets dependent on the importation of U.S. goods. High wages in Canada were also an incentive for U.S. firms to invade the Canadian markets.

American Media and Cultural Influences

As Hiller notes in his analysis of Canadian Society, perhaps no institution has a more powerful role in forging a national identity than the media. Many Canadians express as much concern over the penetration of American media—and through it, American culture—as they do over American economic penetration. Because of the proximity of the United States, U.S. media are immediately accessible and its cultural influences are strong (although cultural influences from Britain and France are felt also). The concern is that the U.S. influence will distort Canadian values and sense of identity. Indeed, studies suggest that many Canadians see their society through the eyes of the U.S. media as having characteristics like those of their neighbor, especially as being violent and aggressive. In addition, the larger U.S. market enables U.S. media companies to produce their programs for less than Canadian producers can produce programs. For example, it is often cheaper for the Canadian television networks—the publicly owned CBC and the privately owned CTV—to purchase rights to programs from one of the U.S. networks than to produce their own. The paradox is that although Canadians are concerned about these cultural influences, they enjoy watching American television, listening to American music artists, and going to American movies.

The issue is not so much whether foreign media and cultural influences should be allowed into Canada as whether their presence retards the development of an indigenous Canadian culture. To guarantee against such an outcome, the federal government pursues several policies aimed at strengthening Canadian culture and its media outlets. For example, the government subsidizes many cultural activities, from symphony orchestras to the film industry. But the most controversial policy aims at increasing the Canadian content of cultural activities by requiring the media—be it television or orchestra—to include a certain proportion of original Canadian content in their programming and to use Canadian artists whenever possible. As Hiller notes, despite these controversial elements of forced-choice in this policy, the Canadian public has supported it as a way of protecting Canadian culture.

Summary

The concern in Canada over its national identity has long been tied to the fear of having the Canadian identity and sovereignty swallowed up by the United States. This concern recently culminated in the 1988 federal parliamentary election, the most bitterly contested in Canadian history, which amounted to a referendum on the 1988 Free Trade Agreement between the United States and Canada. The governing Progressive Conservatives had earlier signed the pact, which would reduce or eliminate remaining tariffs on goods (about 20 percent) traded between the two countries over a ten-year period (tariffs on the other 80 percent of goods traded had previously been eliminated). Despite the Conservatives large majority in the House of Commons, strong opposition from the Liberal and New Democratic parties as well as from segments of the public forced the Conservatives to call the election. Victory for the Conservatives would be a mandate for the agreement; their defeat would shelve it.

Opposition to the pact was not centered on the principle of free trade but on other provisions in the pact that many Canadians saw as a threat to their economic and political independence. These provisions would eliminate barriers to U.S. investment in Canada and to free trade in agriculture and energy, as well as open up a free market in service industries. Opponents of the agreement feared that American interests could buy up the remaining Canadian industries that they did not already own, as well as Canada's huge natural resources, particularly energy. Canadians also feared that their universal health care system would be threatened if American private, for-profit hospitals were allowed to operate in Canada and compete with the nonprofit, public system. In addition, the pact called for "harmonization" of the two countries' economies. This provision was widely interpreted in Canada as meaning that the United States could object to

Canadian content requirements as unfair restraint of trade and could even veto Canadian social programs, including national health care and equalization payments to poorer provinces, as "unfair subsidies" to Canadian industries. Canadians also feared that such harmonization would override Canada's tougher environmental laws, such as those that deal with acid rain.

The election was held on 21 November 1988. Although the Conservatives won a majority of seats in the House and immediately began to implement the pact, the issues raised in the election were not entirely settled. The Conservatives had received only 43 percent of the popular vote in a three-way contest; the other 57 percent went to the Liberal Party or the NDP—parties that had bitterly opposed the treaty.

Continued widespread opposition to the treaty may have played a significant role in the unprecedented defeat of the Conservatives in the 1993 federal elections (along with economic recession, the highest per capita national debt in the industrial world and the unpopular "goods and service tax"—a type of federal value-added or sales tax). From a majority government before the election, the Conservatives were reduced to holding just *two* seats in Parliament after the election. Ironically, however, the newly elected majority Liberal government, which had continued to oppose the free trade agreement, not only did not void this agreement, but went on to sign the more far-reaching North American Free Trade Agreement (NAFTA) with the United States and Mexico. Since many of the provisions of the FTA and NAFTA do not go into effect until 2000, it is still too early to say how free trade will affect Canadian identity or sovereignty.

Conclusions

This monograph began by raising the question of whether there is a "Canadian society" in the sociological sense of the term. Do the cultural groups and regions in Canada adhere to the same sets of institutions, values, and identity? And are these institutions, values, and identity distinct from those of other societies so as to be expressive of an entity that is uniquely "Canadian"?

The evidence surveyed here suggests mixed trends regarding cohesion. Canada's underlying linguistic fault line has recently reemerged as a chasm. Failure of negotiations aimed at getting Quebec to sign the new constitution, the reelection of the Parti Quebecois and its promise of a second referendum on Quebec sovereignty constitute critical challenges to Canada's social cohesion and political sovereignty. Another threat comes from the increased autonomy of provincial governments, and demands for more autonmy—not only from Quebec, but from western provinces as well. However, regional economic inequalities have diminished, especially between western and central Canada, while new communication and transportation technologies have increased linkages among Canada's regions. Moreover, what is to be made of the presence of regional parties in the federal parliament? Do parties like Reform and Bloc Quebecois represent an increased threat to national sovereignty, or do they represent greater symbolic commitment to that sovereignty (even if unintentionally, as in the case of the Bloc Quebecois)?

Trends are also mixed with respect to the distinctiveness of Canadian society. Over the past generation, the state has been increasingly employed to create and maintain Canadian distinctiveness, such as in policies requiring Canadian content and limiting foreign ownership. National symbols, such as the flag and the national anthem have been created, and the constitution officially adopted, or "patriated." However, many of these symbols are threatened. Canada's slow-growing economy and massive federal budget deficit threaten social programs such as national health care and provincial equalization payments. Canada's oldest national symbol, the transcontinental railroad, has already been dismantled as a cost saving move by the federal government. Free trade and increased economic integration with the United States will make it harder to restrict U.S. economic and cultural influences.

Moreover, increased economic ties with the United States could further undermine the forces of cohesion. By reducing the perception of an American threat, economic integration could weaken the incentives for regional and language group accommodations that were so strong in the founding of the Canadian Confederation in the 1860s. Free trade and guaranteed access to U.S. markets could also weaken preceptions, in Quebec and elsewhere, of the economic necessity of staying in Canada.

Ultimately, the cohesiveness and distinctiveness of Canadian society will be affected by the 1982 constitution and the eventual outcome of negotiations over constitutional reform. It could be argued that the underlying purpose of the constitution is to increase cohesion by providing a distinctive statement of fundamental principles that all Canadians could embrace. In particular, the guarantee of individual and minority group rights in the constitution's Charter of Rights and Freedoms provides a clear commitment to the principles of tolerance and multiculturalism—or what sociologist Harry Hiller has called "polycentric" nationalism. Additionally, individual rights and multiculturalism were institutionalized in the constitution as part of a strategy to help counterbalance and diffuse the fundamental conflict between French and English. The constitution transformed the dynamics of ethic politics from its bilingual and bicultural basis by legitimating the emergence of "new groups"—such as women, the disabled, immigrant ethnic minorities—and "new" old groups—Native Peoples. The constitution gave voice to the concerns of these groups and to their greater participation in decsionmaking processes.

However, the initial effects of this transformation would seem to have increased social fragmentation rather than cohesion. The inclusion of new groups with new demands has complicated the traditional process of accomodations between Quebec and the rest of Canada. Thus, constitutional reform efforts that began with Meech Lake initiated debate over who is entitled to what consitutional rights and protections. This debate, in turn, has led to a myriad of devolutionist demands, including the proposal in the Charlottetown Accord for a "third tier" of governments to provide autonomy for the various Native Peoples within existing provinces and territories. While that proposal died along with the Charlottetown Accord, agreement was reached in 1994 to split the vast Northwest Territories by creating a home for Inuits, called Nunavut, in the eastern two-thirds. This split will begin in 1999 and be completed in 2008. It is yet to be decided what will happen to the remaining territory, but half a dozen Native groups are vying for the creation of similar autonomous regions.

In light of these recent trends and events, it might seem to many outside Canada-and especially to Americans—that Canadian society is extremely fragile and its future highly problematic. However, it must be remembered that Canada is almost a hundred years younger than the United States. And, whereas, the Revolution gave American society an immediate sense of identity and many of its national symbols, such as the flag, many other symbols came much later. For example, the "Star Spangled Banner," became the national anthem only in this century. It must also be remembered that the establishment of these national symbols and the enshrinement of basic principles into the U.S. Constitution did not eliminate internal conflicts and create social cohesion. Indeed, it was some ninety years after the signing of the Constitution, and only after a long and bloody civil war, that America's most divisive social issue—slavery—was "settled." But the racial divisions from that earlier period continue to this day.

This last point suggests that it is the building of any cohesive, distinct society that is fragile and problematic, not just Canada's. Indeed, "nation building" is everywhere a gradual process, a process that is probably never fully complete, and a process that is by no means unidirectional. Today, the issues that make that process fragile in Canada are also divisive issues in American society: in particular, free trade and multiculturalism.

Does this process of nation building in the late twentieth century go against the trend toward the creation of a world economy, in which capital and commodities flow freely across national boundaries? Does nationalism stifle the economic prosperity of citizens by restricting this flow, or does it protect them from the uncertainties of the world market? To a great extent, these were the underlying issues in the Canadian debate over the 1988 Free Trade Agreement. And these were issues that were echoed point by point in the American debate over NAFTA in 1993.

Does multiculturalism and demands for self-determination by various "minority" groups threaten the cohesion of modern societies and inevitably lead to violent fragmentaion, as in the former Soviet Union and Yugoslavia, or Northern Ireland? Does the mandating of group-based rights, entitlements, and protections erode individual rights that are seen as fundamental for democratic society? Are laws and policies mandating assimilation and conformity to "traditional" social values any less divisive and authoritarian? While it may seem that these issues are more sharply drawn in Canada, they are not uniquely Canadian. One has only to look at recent American policy-making—on the one hand restricting "hate speech" and promoting "multicultural" curricula in schools, but on the other requiring the learning of English and the teaching of "the superiority of American society"—to recognize that these are common concerns in a changing world.

Bibliography

Brym, Robert J. 1978. "Regional Social Structure and Agrarian Radicalism in Canada: Alberta, Saskatchewan and New Brunswick." *Canadian Review of Sociology and Anthropology* 15:339-51.

Carroll, William K., John Fox, and Michael D. Ornstein. 1982. "The Network of Directorate Links among the Largest Canadian Firms." *Canadian Review of Sociology and Anthropology* 19:44-69.

Fenwick, Rudy. 1981. "Social Change and Ethnic Nationalism: An Historical Analysis of the Separatist Movement in Quebec." *Comparative Studies in Society and History* 23:196-216.

Floras, Augie. 1989. "Toward a Multicultural Reconstruction of Canadian Society." *The American Review of Canadian Studies.* 19:307-20.

Gibbins, Roger. 1980. *Prairie Politics and Society: Regionalism in Decline.* Toronto: Butterworth.

Hiller, Harry H. 1986. *Canadian Society: A Macro Analysis.* Scarborough, Ont.: Prentice-Hall.

Johnson, Richard, Andre Blais, Henry E. Brady, and Jean Crete. 1991. "Free Trade and the Dynamics of the 1988 Canadian Election. In *The Ballot and It's Message: Voting in Canada,* edited by Joseph Wearing. Toronto: Copp Clark Pitman.

Laxer, Gordon. 1985. "Foreign Ownership and Myths about Canadian Development." *Canadian Review of Sociology and Anthropology* 22:311-45.

Lipset, Seymour Martin. 1986. "Historical Traditions and National Characteristics: A Comparative Analysis of Canada and the United States." *Canadian Journal of Sociology* 11:113-55.

Macpherson, C. B. 1962. *Democracy in Alberta: Social Credit and the Party System.* Toronto: University of Toronto Press.

McRae, Kenneth. 1974. "Consociationalism and the Canadian Political System." In *Consociational Democracy: Political Accommodation in Segmented Societies,* edited by Kenneth McRae, 238-61. Toronto: McClelland and Stewart.

McRoberts, Kenneth, and Patrick J. Monahan, editors. 1993. *The Charlottetown Accord, the Referendum and the Future of Canada.* Toronto: University of Toronto Press.

Milner, Henry. 1977. "The Decline and Fall of the Quebec Liberal Regime: Contradictions in the Modern Quebec State." In *The Canadian State: Political Economy and Political Power,* edited by Leo Panitch, 101-32. Toronto: University of Toronto Press.

Panitch, Leo. 1981. "Dependency and Class in Canadian Political Economy." *Studies in Political Economy* 6:7-33.

Pinard, Maurice, and Richard F. Hamilton. 1984. "The Class Bases of the Quebec Independence Movement: Conjectures and Evidence." *Ethnic and Racial Studies* 7:19-54.

Porter, John. 1965. *The Vertical Mosaic.* Toronto: University of Toronto Press.

Smith, Joel, and David K. Jackson. 1981. *Restructuring the Canadian State: Prospects for Three Political Scenarios.* Durham, N.C.: Duke University Center International Studies.

Truman, Tom. 1971. "A Critique of Seymour M. Lipset's Article, 'Value Differences, Absolute or Relative: The English-Speaking Democracies.'" *Canadian Journal of Political Science* 4:497-525.

Weaver, R. Kent, ed. 1992. *The Collapse of Canada.* Washington, D.C.: The Brookings Institution.